IMAGES
of America

J.M. Davis Arms and Historical Museum

This is the first-known photograph of James Monroe Davis, taken after his first visit to Claremore, Oklahoma, in 1916. He was 29 years old.

On the Cover: Collector J.M. Davis was a familiar sight behind the registration desk at the Mason Hotel. Davis owned and operated the hotel from 1916 to 1973

IMAGES
of America

J.M. DAVIS ARMS AND HISTORICAL MUSEUM

Larry Larkin, Wayne McCombs,
and John Wooley

ARCADIA
PUBLISHING

ISBN 978-1-4671-0404-3

Published by Arcadia Publishing
Charleston, South Carolina

Printed in the United States of America

Library of Congress Control Number: 2019936487

For all general information, please contact Arcadia Publishing:
Telephone 843-853-2070
Fax 843-853-0044
E-mail sales@arcadiapublishing.com
For customer service and orders:
Toll-Free 1-888-313-2665

Visit us on the Internet at www.arcadiapublishing.com

Contents

ACKNOWLEDGMENTS

Any work of this nature is a collaborative effort, and the authors want to take this opportunity to thank all the people who generously shared their time and memories, helped with research, contributed photographs or memorabilia, or aided us in other ways with the assembly of the original book, as well as those who came aboard for this special 50th anniversary edition. We are especially grateful to Jim Batchelder, John Cary, Patt Cameron, April Churchill, the *Claremore Daily Progress*, Debi Corley-Workman, Dell David, Dr. C.K. Doran, Linda Faulkner, Judy Eagleton, Alyne Good Eilnad, Martin Good, Susan Ellerbach, William R. Higgins, Debbie Jackson, Shirley Johnson, Dorothy Kizer-Dennis, Shirley McClurg, Clay McIntosh, Donna McSpadden, Rick Mosier, the Mickey Perry family, Hilary Pittman, Stanley Prather, Frank C. Robson, the Rogers County Historical Society, Jane Sallee, Jason Schubert, Shirley Taylor, the *Tulsa World*, and the University of Tulsa, Special Collections, McFarlin Library.

We gratefully acknowledge Jonnie Neely for her generous gift in memory of her late husband, Paul E. Neely, and in honor of the Neely family. Her gift has made this special 50th anniversary edition a reality. Through many years of service, the Neely family has greatly contributed to the culture, daily life, and community spirit of Claremore and Rogers County.

Unless otherwise noted, all images are courtesy of the J.M. Davis Arms and Historical Museum.

Pictured on Thanksgiving Day 2018 is the family of Paul E. Neely (insert). Family members are, from left to right, (first row) Elliot Neely and Emmalynn Neely; (second row) Knox Keeney, Neely Holley, Jonnie Neely, Reed Holley, and Wyatt Ball; (third row) Aaron Ball, Kellie Ball, Crystle Keeney, Ed Barstow, Sherry Barstow, Terrie Neely, Steve Neely, Ginger Kollmann, Dave Kollmann, Amy Neely, and Ryan Neely; (fourth row) Brian Ball, Brandon Ball, Westin Clinton, Grant Holley, and Jack Keeney.

Introduction

In 2019, one of the American Southwest's great attractions, the J.M. Davis Arms and Historical Museum in Claremore, Oklahoma, turned a half-century old—no small feat in this time of disposable culture and its here-today, gone-tomorrow diversions. As impressive as that run is, however, it is only part of the story. The origins of this one-of-a-kind historical repository go back well beyond those 50 years, to the first third of the last century, when Claremore was a vacation destination famed for its restorative mineral water baths and a remarkable man named J.M. Davis was not only mayor of the thriving town but also owner of a main street establishment, the Mason Hotel.

Like other famed personalities from Claremore, including American icon Will Rogers, playwright and poet Lynn Riggs, and recording artist Patti Page, J.M. Davis was an extraordinary figure who left a lasting impact. His particular immortality comes from his single-minded dedication to amassing, as a sign atop the hotel's entrance in the mid-1900s put it, the "Greatest Collection of Guns in the World"—and his insistence that anyone who wanted to see and study it could do so free of charge.

Those intrigued enough to go through the doors of the Mason Hotel from the late 1920s through most of the 1960s, including many curious folks from faraway states and even distant countries, never went away disappointed. Once inside, visitors would immediately find themselves in another world, surrounded by a jaw-dropping number of firearms and other items displayed on the walls and in the hotel's ballroom, sweeping through the hallways and the coffee shop, taking up every spare bit of room in the place. They would also usually find the man who had pieced together this panorama of weaponry—a calm, businesslike Arkansas native who had traded a couple of thousand acres of timberland in his home state for Claremore's Mason Hotel back in the 1910s.

In fact, he could often be found behind the registration desk, ready to rent a room, to talk about his vast collection, or to do both.

His full name was John Monroe Davis. Born in Union County, Arkansas, in 1887 to children of Danish and Irish immigrants, he was the eighth of nine children in a farming family. In the booklet *John Monroe Davis: From Hobby to Legacy*, published in the late 1990s, author Patt Cameron described the beginning of Davis's passion for guns:

> He was always a sickly child and as a result, very spoiled. He hated school because he couldn't play games like other boys. Finally, he rebelled, so his father took him out of school and put him to work on his 400 acre timber plantation. When the doctor said his health was so bad that he wouldn't survive without the medicine that he refused to take, his father offered him a small 410 gauge shotgun that J.M. had been wanting. . . . J.M. agreed to stop fussing and take the medicine. That was the beginning of a 20,000 firearms and related items collection.

He was seven years old when his dad gave him the shotgun that set him on the path that would make his name famous. And that .410, added Cameron, was not only the first weapon J.M. Davis collected; it remained his favorite of them all.

An early tragedy may also have spurred young Davis's passion for acquiring and collecting firearms. Four years after he had received the .410, his father, also named John, died. For her book on J.M. Davis's first wife, *A Portrait of Addie: The Woman Behind the Man Behind the Guns*, published in 1998 by Lifestyles Press, Kathryn Davis interviewed Davis's nephew Dr. Randolph Murray, who told her, "He [Davis] worked on the farm but his main interest was guns. His father had left him his 12-gauge, double-barreled shotgun. Then Uncle Monroe started looking for different kinds of guns, so my mother told me, and he was never happy unless he was looking at or talking about guns."

It would take him the better part of three more decades, but J.M. Davis finally got to do what made him the happiest.

The route to Claremore and the beginning of his exhibition of firearms was a circuitous one for Davis, taking him from the family farm to Arkansas's Mount Magazine Military Academy and from there to Draughn's Business College in Texas, where he met future wife Addie Lee Smith. They were married December 4, 1910, in Texarkana.

According to *John Monroe Davis: From Hobby to Legacy*, Davis was doing well in the timber business, making and selling railroad ties, when he and his wife "read about oil gushing in and around Tulsa, Oklahoma." Claremore was located just down the road from Tulsa, and when the two came to the area to check things out for themselves, they stayed at Claremore's Mason Hotel. It happened to be for sale by its owner, Dr. John Rucker, and it looked like a good deal to J.M. and Addie Davis.

So, Davis and Dr. Rucker struck a bargain that involved prime timberland back in Davis's own state. That was in 1916. A year later, Davis and his wife were living in Claremore and operating the hotel formerly owned by Dr. Rucker, who had received some good land in exchange.

Davis soon became a town leader, with the Mason Hotel Coffee Shop a meeting place for Claremore's businesspeople and elected officials. He began his first of six terms as mayor in 1921, only four years after arriving in the city to stay.

It took longer for Davis to start displaying his collection in the hotel. When he finally did, in 1929, he was exactly one firearm shy of 100. But the 99 pieces he put up in the lobby immediately began attracting attention—and, of course, offers from gun owners looking to sell him their own weapons or even to trade for something they had seen on the hotel walls.

According to his sister Myrtha Duty, Addie Davis was an integral part in the whole operation from the beginning, including the exhibits. "Addie was . . . the real backbone of the Mason Hotel as well as the gun collection," Duty told *A Portrait of Addie* author Clausen. "She limited the amount which Monroe could spend on guns to $2,000 per month, and she steered him like a captain steers his ship, always trying to keep him out of rough water."

His monthly allowance could buy a lot of things, however, especially during the Great Depression and the Dust Bowl, and even with that restriction on his spending, Davis found his collection growing exponentially. As more and more people came to him with intriguing pieces, the shotguns, pistols, and rifles that decorated the hotel's interior were joined by other collectibles. He began picking up related items, like knives and swords. He acquired American Indian artifacts and displayed them next to saddles, music boxes, political buttons, and World War I posters. He also amassed an impressive number of beer steins, John Rogers statuary, and animal heads and horns. While trading, selling, and buying, Davis made sure to keep much of his unique and irreplaceable treasure trove before the people, filing every wall and hallway in the place before seeing it overflow into several private rooms.

His most impressive single purchase came in the early 1940s, when he made a deal with a man named Merle Gill, formerly of the Kansas City Police Department, to buy a collection that became Davis's Gallery of Outlaw Guns. Gill had collected them during the 1920s and 1930s—the heyday of the middle-American outlaw—and exhibited them throughout the country at fairs and carnivals. The collection remains one of the most popular attractions at the J.M. Davis Arms and Historical Museum.

In the late 1940s, a few years after he'd served his last term as Claremore's mayor, Davis first began talking with city officials and others about a museum to house his collection, which, at the time, included thousands of items and had become known worldwide. It was not until the early 1960s when the J.M. Davis Foundation, the entity that led to the construction of the J.M. Davis Arms and Historical Museum, was created. Davis was nearly 80 years old at the time. He had married his second wife, the former Genevieve Breeden, four years earlier, following Addie's 1959 death. And he was still working the registration desk at the Mason Hotel, patiently answering the questions of those encountering his exhibits for the first time, and still dealing in new acquisitions for his collection.

"He couldn't believe all the people who'd sent him different things," recalls Claremore resident Jim Batchelder, who first visited the Mason Hotel as a youngster in the early 1960s. "It wasn't all guns. It was swords, knives, beer steins, and that's how the collection grew—things came from all over the world."

Like many visitors both young and old, the teenaged Batchelder became entranced with the Davis collection. "It fascinated Mr. Davis, and it fascinated me," Batchelder remembers. "I was so fascinated that every time I got the chance, I would go down there and hang around all the time. He'd be sitting in his chair right behind the desk—he could barely see over the top of the counter—and every time I walked up to talk to him, he'd smile at me and say, 'Thank you for finding the time to come back.'"

Within the space of a few years, Batchelder and many others, both in and out of Claremore, who loved spending time with Davis's collection would see it moved to a different and more secure location only a few blocks away.

"Mr. Davis had long had his dream of getting a permanent place to house his collection," notes Wayne McCombs, the museum's executive director. "He wanted it to be able to be enjoyed by people for many, many years to come."

That process began in earnest in the spring of 1965, when Davis transferred ownership of his whole collection to the J.M. Davis Foundation, which in turn leased it to the State of Oklahoma for a 99-year period with an option to renew. The cost to the state was $1, which Davis refused to take.

"He committed the lease with two preemptive provisions," says noted Claremore rancher and businessman Frank Robson. "The first was that a suitable building had to be built to house the museum, in a location that he would approve of. The second thing was, nobody could be charged for an entry to the museum, because he didn't want anybody not to see the display because of their economic conditions."

It took three more years before the first phase of the museum was completed. The Oklahoma Legislature had to approve funding, property had to be purchased, the museum building had to be designed, and bids had to be taken for its construction. It was not until early 1968 that the first spade of dirt was turned on the lot that would become the museum's home.

Davis's hometown newspaper, the *Claremore Progress*, ran a January 14 story under a headline that summed the situation up nicely: "Dream's End Reached At Groundbreaking." An unnamed reporter wrote the following:

> A project dating back to about 1952 became a dream's end Saturday when J.M. Davis and his wife turned the first spade of dirt at [the] site of the museum to hold his gun collection.
>
> Rep. Bill Briscoe, during the formal ceremonies, related efforts begun by Joe Zodrow, then manager of the Chamber of Commerce, and former Chamber president Ed Livermore, publisher and then editor of the *Progress*.
>
> Briscoe said the two men then talked to Davis, who owns the Mason Hotel where the guns are now housed, about the building of a museum for the world's largest collection of guns, as well as other historical artifacts.
>
> The representative related how that effort, and several since, failed mainly due to lack of funds necessary to construct a suitable facility.
>
> Master of Ceremonies was Clem McSpadden, president pro tempore of the state senate . . .
>
> The museum, to be constructed with state funds, will be operated by the state with no admission charge to the public . . .

The first section of the museum, featuring some 5,000 firearms and several thousand other artifacts, opened to the public on June 27, 1969, Davis's 82nd birthday. As is the case with most projects of this stature, there had been challenges right up until the time the doors opened. One of them, which ultimately did not materialize, involved nothing less than the jailing of Davis himself. It happened as he was transferring each item in his collection to the museum, a time-consuming, painstaking process. Frank Robson explains:

> In the spring [of 1968], they passed a law that said all automatic weapons had to be registered and the information given to the federal government through the ATF. And the situation was that Mr. Davis had all these guns on the walls downstairs, but he had thousands of guns stored in crates upstairs.
>
> At that point in time, Mr. Davis was still clerking in the hotel behind that little desk he had. And an ATF agent for the Tulsa area came by and told him he had to have all his automatic weapons registered by this date.
>
> Mr. Davis told him, "Yes, we're very aware of the law, and what we're doing is, we're registering these guns as we come to them."
>
> The guy said, "I don't think you understand, Mr. Davis. Your guns have to be registered by this date."
>
> "Well, we understand that," Mr. Davis said. "We're going to obey the law. We are going to register these guns as we come to them, and we don't intend to hire a whole group of people to go up and go through all those cases of guns and sort them out." He would've had to hire about a hundred people to go upstairs and pick out all the automatic weapons.
>
> And this fellow said, "I don't think you understand the law."
>
> "This is what we're going to do," Mr. Davis said, "and we're going to abide by the law."

Eventually, Robson notes, the ATF agent got his supervisor to go to the hotel, and when Davis patiently explained to the man how he was doing things, he got his boss to come up from Dallas. Davis, unwavering, told the bigwig the same thing.

"This guy got irate," remembers Robson. "His blood pressure went up, and he said, 'Well, let me tell you what we're going to do to you! We're going to put you in jail!'"

Today, the J.M. Davis Arms and Historical Museum rivals the venerable Will Rogers Memorial Museum as Claremore's top tourist attraction. An estimated 30,000 visitors a year, from all across the globe, come to witness for themselves the largest private collection of firearms in the world. These pieces, which number more than 13,000 are the shining stars in a stellar lineup of some 50,000 artifacts on display.

Spreading over most of an acre, the Davis Museum features more than a mile of gun exhibits alone. Over the years, it has also been home for many special exhibitions; recent ones include a group of original World War I recruitment posters accompanied by a locally produced seven-minute documentary and, beginning in 2019, a display of the .38 caliber Winchester used by banker W.J. Myers to shoot and kill the notorious Indian Territory outlaw Henry Starr (who, coincidentally, lived the last part of his life in Davis's Mason Hotel).

In addition to firearm aficionados, the museum also regularly draws scholars and historians. Its reference library and meeting room are often used by those doing weapons-related and other historical research.

First and foremost, however, the J.M. Davis Gun Museum remains a unique historical attraction, a dazzling display of weaponry and other memorabilia from America's past.

As the museum's executive director Wayne McCombs puts it, "Thanks to the State of Oklahoma, the citizens of Claremore, and the thousands and thousands of people from all over who've enjoyed and supported us, Mr. Davis's dream has been kept alive for the past fifty years. We hope and believe that this first half-century is only the beginning."

That sentiment is echoed regularly by the comments in the visitors' log and the notes and messages received by the staff members. A visitor from Michigan recently summed up the appeal of the place in a handwritten note. "This," it read, "is positively the BEST MUSEUM in the nation!"

One

John Monroe Davis, A Born Collector 1887–1929

The .410 muzzle-loading shotgun J.M. Davis received at the age of seven was an outright bribe from his father, who was trying to make the willful child swallow the medicine necessary to save his life. According to author Patt Cameron, J.M.'s dad had offered him just about everything, including "the best pony on the farm," before the weapon did the trick.

It did more than that. The gun, which some sources say was worth about $1.50, started him on the road to an irreplaceable collection valued at more than $7 million, growing to such a size that a museum would have to be built around it. Even at an early age, J.M. Davis was someone who knew what he wanted, and what it would take to get it. When he and his wife, Addie, arrived in Claremore for the first time, less than a decade after Oklahoma's statehood, he decided that he not only liked the area, he also liked the hotel where they stayed. The same year, he acquired it and soon had moved to the northeastern Oklahoma town from his native Arkansas.

The .410 had started Davis on the road to collecting weaponry, and his passion for the hobby continued to grow. Luckily for him, he was able to indulge his interests, making a good living not only from the hotel but also from his construction business. With the oil industry booming around Claremore, workers needed places to stay, and between the homes he was building and the rooms of his hotel, Davis had them covered.

When Davis decided to display the pieces he'd collected on the walls of the Mason Hotel, he'd acquired a total of 99 firearms. It was an impressive number, but only a tiny fraction of the more than 20,000 he'd come to own, sharing walls and shelves and unoccupied rooms in the hotel with several thousand other collectors' items.

In 1882, what was to become the city of Claremore organized around a stop for the St. Louis & San Francisco Railroad, later known simply as the Frisco, in Indian Territory. As Claremore begin to grow from a sleepy farming community to a bustling town, the Frisco not only allowed its residents and visitors to travel north and south with ease, but also gave area businesses the opportunity to obtain merchandise much easier and faster than before.

It did not take long before the Frisco drew some competition in Claremore. Around the beginning of the 20th century, the Missouri Pacific & Iron Mountain Railroad also built a depot there, making Claremore one of the few towns in Oklahoma that could claim two railroad lines. One of the reasons was the radium-water springs around the city. People from all over the United States would ride in to take the town's famous radium baths, which were believed to have restorative powers. Later, Claremore favorite son Will Rogers would often write and talk about Claremore's remarkable healing waters.

When this c. 1900 photograph of the town's Main Street was taken, Claremore was still a horse-and-buggy community. The first automobile would not show up in town for several more years. Today, this area lies at the corner of two streets named in honor of a pair of the city's most famous citizens: Will Rogers Boulevard (formerly Main Street) and J.M. Davis Boulevard.

This photograph from the same time period is looking to the west instead of the east, as is the case in the top photograph. This is the present-day corner of Cherokee Street and Will Rogers Boulevard. Some two decades after the arrival of the Frisco rail stop, Claremore had grown into a thriving city, its residents justifiably proud of Main Street's new brick buildings.

Clement Vann Rogers established the First National Bank in Claremore in 1884, seen in this 1907 photograph, two years after the Frisco Railroad added its Claremore depot. Rogers was a well-known man in Indian Territory. He was a rancher, Cherokee senator, and judge who would help write the constitution for the State of Oklahoma. In the 1920s and 1930s, his son Will would become one of the most famous men in America.

Clem Rogers's First National Bank was on the west end of what would later be known as the Mason Block, named after the hotel that spread across it. When this 1909 photograph was taken, the Claremore mayor's office was located on the second floor of the bank building. Those with sharp eyes will be able to see mayor Joe LaHay peering out his office window, perhaps wondering what a cameraman is doing on the Main Street of his town.

This 1906 shot faces west, where the Lindell Hotel can be seen in the middle of the block. Following the opening of the Mason Hotel in January 1910, that block would be the downtown area known to residents as the Mason Block.

Another hotel that sprung up during Claremore's early days was the Elk, pictured in 1909. It lay just to the west of the Lindell. This part of downtown was an especially popular location for a hotel; the Frisco depot was located only one half-block to the south.

Although one could assume that the Hotel Main was named for its location on Claremore's Main Street, it was in fact the namesake of its owner, William Main. The Main would prove to be one of the city's longest standing buildings, lasting until J.M. Davis bought out the entire block many years later. Meanwhile, in 1909, partners J.P. Mason and E.M. Brown leased the east half of that block and began building the Mason Hotel. This May 1910 photograph is the earliest known taken of the Mason, four months after the official opening.

The east end of the Mason Block contained a space for businesses to lease. When this 1912 photograph was taken, that business was Walker Brothers Furniture, a locally owned outfit that remained a part of the Claremore scene for decades in various locations. Even though automobiles were making inroads at the time, one can see that the horse and buggy was still a prevalent form of transportation in the growing city.

Six years later, Walker Brothers Furniture had left the Mason Block. They did, however, pave the way for one of the town's first car dealerships, owned by H.J. Platt, who sold Fords. By the time this 1918 photograph was taken, the east corner of the block was one of the busiest areas of commerce in Rogers County. Through the years, a dizzying variety of businesses, including a real estate office, a cigar store, a souvenir jewelry store, and even a city bus station would set up in this location.

The scene in this December 1914 photograph shows the key slots behind the front desk in the lobby of the Mason Hotel. Business must have been good, since there are only a few keys, signifying few unrented rooms. Note also the dapper uniform of the hotel porter. The lobby must have looked very similar to this when Arkansas native J.M. Davis stayed at the Mason on his first Claremore visit in 1916.

Addie Lee Smith was 21 and looking for a job in Texarkana, Texas, when J.M. Davis surprised her with a visit and asked for her hand in marriage. They had become acquainted while students at Draughn's Business College in Tyler, Texas. Addie accepted his proposal, and they were married on Christmas Eve 1910. It was a union that would last until Addie's death in 1959.

At age 17, John Monroe Davis left home to attend Mount Magazine Military Academy, a private institution located in the hills of Arkansas. Of the 300-man student body, some 200 were from other states. In a 1969 interview, Davis told author Kathryn Clausen, "We did a lot of drilling and shooting, as well as studying from books. The teachers were very strict. I became a good marksman. Still am today. I liked drilling and shooting best of all." In later years, countless Oklahoma Military Academy cadets passed in front of his hotel as they walked from their campus to the downtown movie theaters and drugstores. Their ubiquitous presence may have reminded Davis of his own years as a teenage cadet.

His early love for guns helped a young John Monroe Davis recover from an awful mishap. At the age of 15, he accidentally shot and killed his younger brother. In 1969, when he talked to writer Kathryn Clausen, the memory still haunted him. "Byron [Alford] was 12, the baby of the family and much loved by everyone," he told her. "We had just finished eating and we were still at the table. I picked up [my first] gun and was playing with it when it discharged and killed Byron instantly. I didn't know it was loaded. It was a terrible tragedy, which I never really got over. Going off to military school did help, however."

Addie and J.M. not only worked together at the Mason Hotel, they also started a construction company. Addie would buy vacant lots and J.M. would build houses on them. The couple bought a house near the corner of what is now Sixth Street and Lynn Riggs Boulevard and moved in. The lot had plenty of room for another building, so J.M. built his wife her dream home, pictured above. For various reasons, the two never moved in, choosing instead to rent the place. Later, it became the residence of Addie's niece Denyse and her husband, Bob Higgins, who came to Claremore in 1958 to manage the hotel's coffee shop.

J.M. Davis rapidly became a well-respected member of the community. In 1921, only five years after first establishing his residency in Claremore, he entered city politics and won the race for mayor. Although Davis's mayoral office was in this building, which served as Claremore's city hall from 1911 until 1962, those in the know said that more of the town's business was conducted in the Mason Hotel Coffee Shop than ever saw the light of day at city hall.

J.M. and Addie Davis purchased the Mason Hotel well before air-conditioning had become a reality. Claremore historian and longtime Rogers County Clerk Charlie Allton told the authors, "I was the ice man and delivered ice to the hotel. They used a lot of ice in those days."

The three-story Mason didn't have air conditioning, but in 1919, it did get the first elevator in all of Rogers County. Reportedly the 3000th elevator made by the Universal Elevator Company, it had been displayed at the 1904 World's Fair in St. Louis long before Davis purchased it.

SEQUOYAH HOTEL AND RADIUM INSTITUTE, CLAREMORE, OKLA.

In the 1920s, the Mason Hotel's main downtown rival for travelers' trade was the Sequoyah Hotel. Built in 1901, it was located on the southwest corner of Main and Missouri Streets. Radium baths were given on the hotel's second floor beginning in 1905. From 1922 through the mid-1970s, the Sequoyah building housed the First National Bank on its first floor. The drive-through portion of RCB Bank takes up that spot today.

As early as 1926, Addie and J.M. heard that a new hotel was being planned across the street in downtown Claremore. It tuned out to be the Will Rogers, a six-story hotel that contained 78 rooms and seven apartments, with the top floor designed for radium-water bath treatments. The $321,000 hotel opened in January 1930 and dedicated on February 7 of the same year. Will Rogers himself had planned to attend the opening, but a scheduling conflict prevented it. The Rogers County Historical Society and its partners, Community Action Resource and Development and Metro Plains Development, refurbished and reopened the building in 1997. The building, which today is called the Will Rogers Center for Senior Adult Living, looks much the same as it did in 1930.

To help promote Claremore's radium-water treatments to a growing number of tourists, the city's merchants formed the Bath House Radium Water Association, which was the forerunner of today's Claremore Chamber of Commerce. In this 1924 photograph, the members of the association posed in the street in front of the Mason Hotel's porch. J.M. Davis is pictured in the middle in the back, wearing a stylish golfer's cap.

Two

The Greatest Collection of Guns in the World 1930–1965

From 1929 until 1965, when J.M. Davis transferred ownership of his ever-growing collection to the newly formed J.M. Davis Foundation, Inc., the Mason Hotel was the place to go for weapons aficionados from all over. An imposing building that took up nearly a block of the town's Main Street, the 125-room hotel also had a coffee shop that was a favorite meeting place for the locals. Like the rest of the hotel, it was festooned with items from Davis's collection.

After putting those initial 99 weapons on exhibit for the world to see, Davis continued to acquire, catalogue, and display his new acquisitions. In 1930, according to Patt Cameron's *John Monroe Davis: From Hobby to Legacy*, he made his first major purchase of another collection, buying "the famous US Bessette 500-piece collection." In 1932, he bought two more big groups of guns, which gave him a total of some 2,500 weapons, according to Cameron.

An anonymously written booklet that greeted visitors to the museum in the 1970s told of both Davis's collecting patters and his increasing stature among aficionados:

> Mr. Davis collected guns that were unique and different as opposed to specializing in any particular manufacturer or type, making this collection so diversified and educational. He soon became internationally known as a gun expert and avid collector. People came from near and far to buy, sell, trade, or just to get his expert opinion. Well-known authors would seek out Mr. Davis and his collection when writing research books. We find photographs of many guns in this collection included in research material. Mr. Davis loved to collect things and began adding knives, swords, horns, steins, saddles, Indian artifacts, and many other items to his collection of guns.

Those seeking him out to sell, trade, comment on the exhibits, or ask for collecting advice could usually find Davis behind the registration desk of the hotel, as he and Addie continued as hands-on owners.

Although the genesis of the J.M. Davis Arms and Historical Museum goes all the way back to the Arkansas farm of John Monroe Davis's youth, the first public display of his collection came in 1929. That was the year he began mounting his growing collection of firearms in the lobby of his hotel. In addition to drawing tourists and travelers from all across the land, the Mason was also a popular local hangout, with many Claremore residents stopping by regularly to visit and enjoy the ever-expanding collection. The bottom photograph is a close-up view of the display at the Mason Hotel's front desk.

In addition to weaponry, many other items in Davis's collection found their way into the hotel. Addie's favorite collectibles were the antique beer steins, which numbered around 1,500 and were displayed in the coffee shop and dining room. These displays included collectors' items from the German Meissen and Mettlach factories, Prussian Regimental steins, and steins made of old pewter. The smallest held an ounce of liquid; the largest, six gallons.

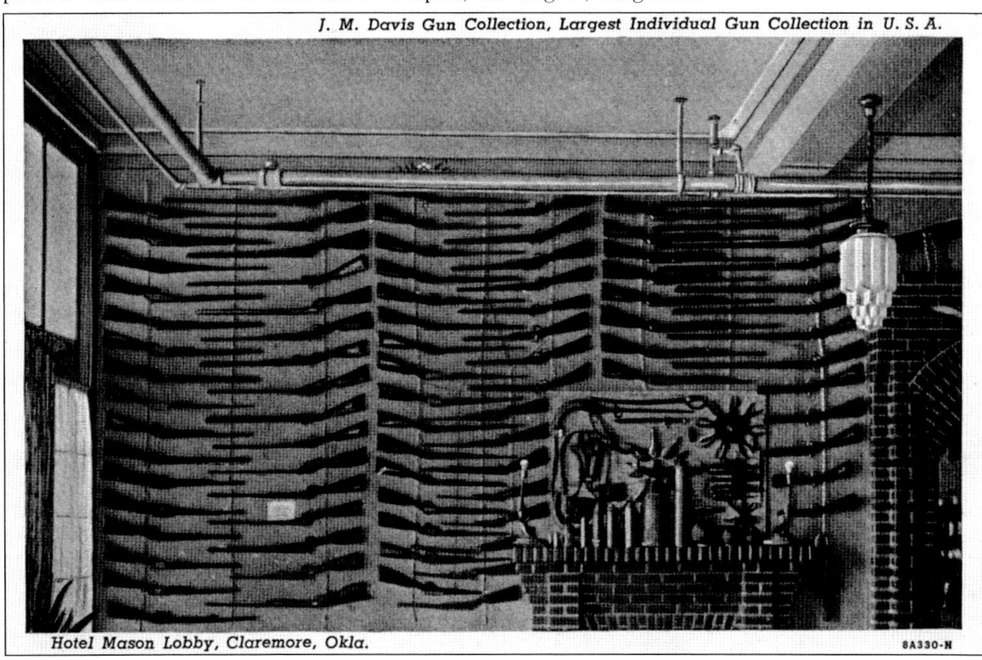

While her husband focused on collecting guns and other artifacts, Addie Davis was in charge of the day-to-day operations of the hotel, hiring all the employees, managing the business, and doing most of the hands-on work. She was active in the Sorosis Club, Delphian Study Club, and the Priscilla Club, as well as a faithful member of Claremore's First Baptist Church. Her friends characterized her as a down-to-earth lady, never putting on airs or trying to impress anyone with her status in the town.

In 1903, the first radium water well was discovered in Claremore. Radium water baths soon developed into a big business, with several hotels offering radium baths. In 1924, a group of Claremore merchants pooled their money and built the most elaborate and largest radium water facility in town, the Radium Bath House, at what is now 330 North Lynn Riggs. It was Claremore's first community-sponsored bathhouse. A newspaper ad of the day read, "Radium Water Baths will improve your health: recommended for rheumatism, stomach troubles, boils, eczema, and other skin diseases." Single baths were $1, and 21 baths were available for $16.50. In addition, massages ranged in price from 50¢ to $3. The Mason Hotel never offered radium treatments, but to compete with the other hotels in town that did, J.M. and Addie Davis bought the Radium Bath House in 1935, along with most of the rest of the block between Fifth and Sixth Streets for $8,000. They also began offering free shuttle service to the bathhouse for their guests. Thirteen years later, in 1948, they sold the building and property for $25,000. Closed in the early 1960s, the bathhouse building was demolished 1967 to make way for the J.M. Davis Arms and Historical Museum.

In the 1930s, America did much of its traveling on passenger trains and cross-country busses. One of the reasons for the success of the Mason Hotel was its location. Not only was the new modern Frisco train station less than a block to the west, the city bus station lay at the east corner of the Mason block. As the 1940s dawned and World War II began, both of these modes of transportation would carry thousands of servicemen across the country.

When J.M. and Addie found out that the Will Rogers Hotel was going up, they decided their own hotel needed a renovation. Over several months in 1926, with Davis doing a great deal of the work himself, they began replacing old furniture with new pieces. Starting on the third floor and going a section at a time, they modernized the rooms by installing bathrooms, new carpet, new curtains, and telephones. Even the hotel's stationary was revamped, and the employees certainly looked sharp in their brand-new uniforms.

The $50,000 refurbishing included a public restroom off the hotel lobby, where overstuffed sofas and chairs along with mahogany tables studded the room. Once the renovations were complete, J.M and Addie Davis held an open house for the citizens of Claremore, who, according to accounts of the time, agreed that the hotel was now fit for royalty.

Overnight guests were able to relax in the second-floor lobby, where they could lounge in oversized chairs, enjoy the piano, and, of course, view displays of the vast Davis collection. The second floor was also home to J.M and Addie Davis, who had a sitting room, bedroom, and bath along with a private kitchen next door. Martha Hill, the hotel's longest-tenured employee, was in charge of the second floor and also served at Addie's personal maid. Born in nearby Talala, she worked at the hotel for almost 40 years, retiring at the age of 85, some 10 years after Addie's death.

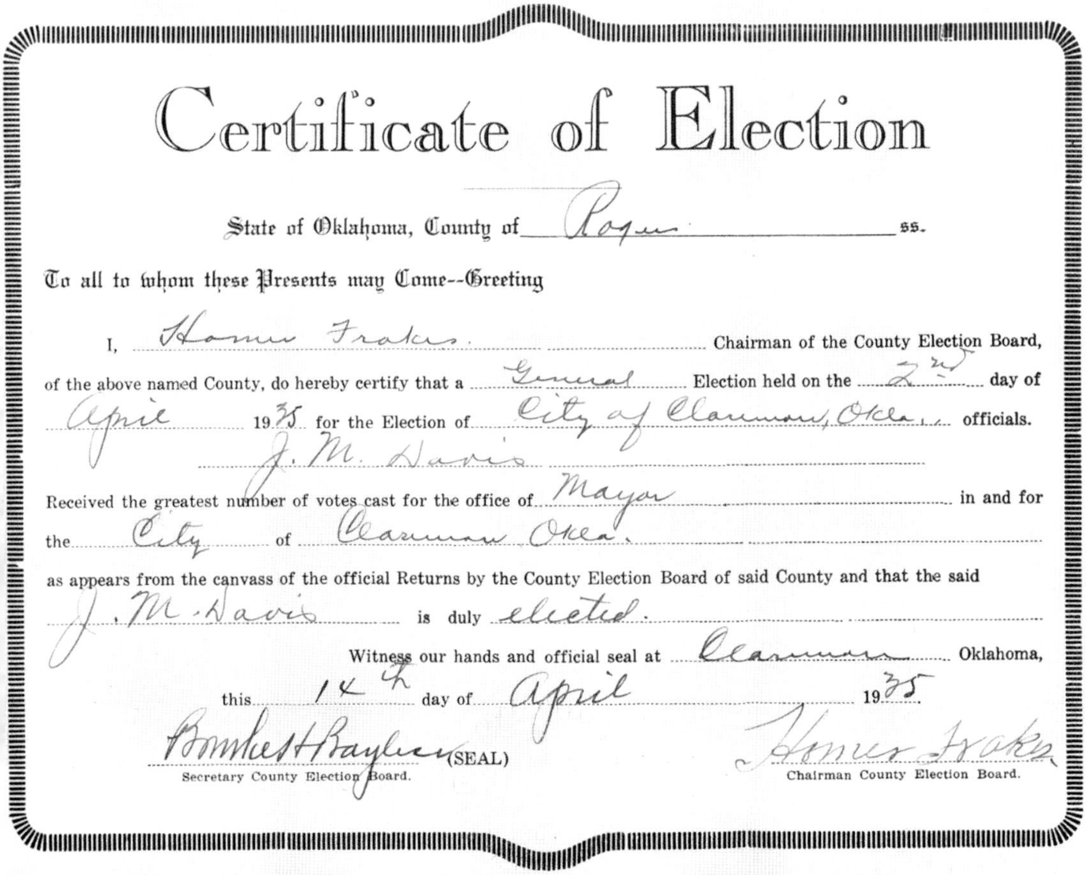

Certificate of Election

State of Oklahoma, County of Rogers ss.

To all to whom these Presents may Come--Greeting

I, Homer Frakes. Chairman of the County Election Board, of the above named County, do hereby certify that a General Election held on the 2nd day of April 1935 for the Election of City of Claremore, Okla. officials.

J. M. Davis

Received the greatest number of votes cast for the office of Mayor in and for the City of Claremore Okla.

as appears from the canvass of the official Returns by the County Election Board of said County and that the said J. M. Davis is duly elected.

Witness our hands and official seal at Claremore Oklahoma,

this 14th day of April 1935

Bomlett Bayless (SEAL)
Secretary County Election Board.

Homer Frakes
Chairman County Election Board.

J.M. Davis served as Claremore's mayor longer than anyone. First elected for a two-year term in 1921, he became mayor again in 1933 and held the office until 1943, or five consecutive terms. Following his years as mayor, he was elected to the city council. His last year in public office was in 1952. This certificate of his election as mayor comes from 1935.

One of the major accomplishments during Davis's years as mayor was the creation of Claremore Lake. Today, it remains the city's main water source as well as a beautiful place for boating, picnicking, and jogging. For years, it has also been the site of the town's Fourth of July fireworks show. In 1940, Davis received a letter from the officer in charge of the US Arms Storehouse in Denver, Colorado, informing him that the storehouse had a French-built Hotchkiss machine gun used by American forces in World War I. The government would ship him the weapon, but only if the mayor of Claremore signed a permit allowing him to keep it. Since Davis was the mayor of Claremore, he signed the necessary paperwork as "Mayor John Davis," and picked up an impressive new piece for his collection. In a 1969 interview, he told writer Kathryn Clausen, "That was one of the most unusual transactions I ever made for a gun."

Another impressive ancillary collection amassed by Davis gathered together several statuettes created by American sculptor John Rogers (no relation to Will Rogers). A self-taught artist from Salem, Massachusetts, in the 1860s Rogers began creating hundreds of lifelike sculptures that were priced within reach of the average citizen. His statues fell into five classes: Civil War subjects; literary topics; theater scenes; domestic-life groups; and historical figures. During his 30-year career, Rogers sold over $1 million worth of molded figurines, although they quickly went out of style and were all but forgotten by the turn of the 20th century. Today, Rogers's statuettes are praised for the delightful sentiment and meticulous care he put into each one. The 26 pieces J.M. Davis was able to purchase over the years are on display today at the Davis Museum.

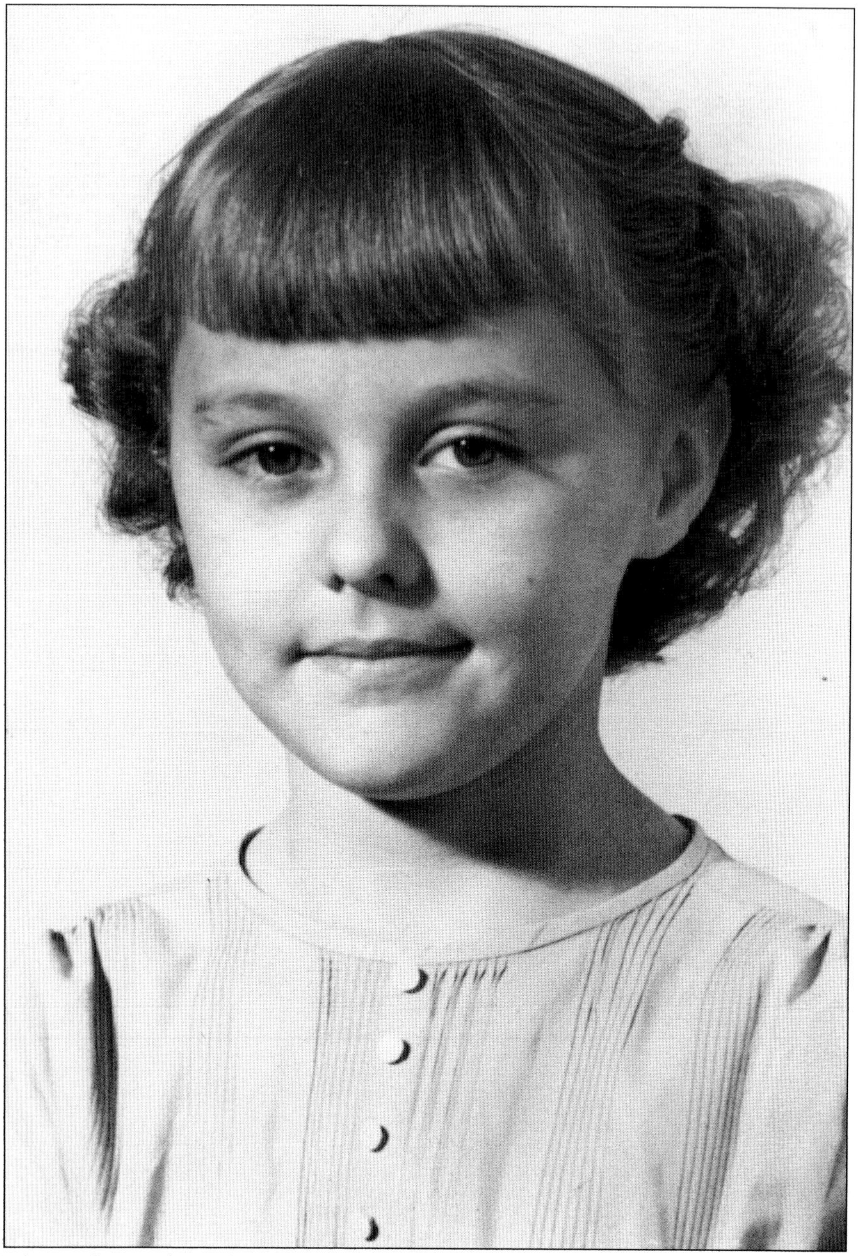

Long before Judy Smith Eagleton started her collection of Claremore memorabilia, she found the Mason Hotel to be a perfect place to "play house" and other children's games. She would get special invitations to come over from J.M. and Addie Davis whenever their young niece Sue Nell Glasby came for a visit. The same age, the two youngsters quickly became good friends. They were usually joined by Georgia Wineinder, who, with her mother, was a permanent resident at the hotel. "I guess we all were nine or 10 the first year," Judy told the authors, "My parents were friends with the Davis family and he thought I would be good company for their niece. Sue Nell, Georgia, and I became good friends right from the start. When Sue Nell was here, I was allowed to refer to them as Uncle Monroe and Aunt Addie. The rest of the time my parents made sure I said Mr. Davis and Mrs. Davis. Both were very kind to me at all times."

When J.M. and Addie Davis took ownership of the hotel, there were two ballrooms. They served as meeting places for many civic clubs, businesses, and private parties. In the 1920s, Davis jazzed up the ballrooms by adding a few animal skins and musical instruments.

As time passed and his collection continued to grow, Davis turned to the ballrooms as places where he could display more memorabilia. As this 1939 photograph indicates, the spaces at first could still be used as a ballroom and dining area. By the early 1950s (see adjoining page), tables and chairs had given way to saddles, cattle horns, and weaponry, the overflow from his collection filling the ballroom and spilling into another packed display room. The only way to navigate through the ballroom now was via a narrow aisle between the heaps of items.

Pictured here is the famous Saddle Room at the Mason Hotel.

Claremore has long loved its parades. In this 1946 photograph, some of the Mason Hotel's guests take advantage of the balcony over the front porch to get a bird's-eye view of the Will Rogers Round-Up Club's rodeo parade.

This late-1940s photograph provides another view of the Mason Hotel. The scene is looking west on Will Rogers Boulevard, which, at the time, marked the end of Claremore's business district.

With 125 rooms, Mason Hotel was the largest hotel in Rogers County. Most rooms had windows that offered good views of downtown activities. The second floor ran the length of the block, and the third floor ran half the way down the block. In this 1942 photograph, the souvenir shop is seen on the east corner. In the 1950s and 1960s, Dave and Norma Collision owned and operated a jewelry and souvenir business there called Dave's Indian Store. "My husband was a horse trader," said Norma Collision years later. "We'd go west and pick up Indian jewelry and artifacts and then we would go east and sell. Then we would pick up products in the east and go west. We drove a Cadillac and we would load it down, and we pulled an eight-foot trailer behind it. Everyone from coast to coast would tell you they knew Dave Collision and his family that drove a yellow 1955 Coupe de Ville Cadillac. We had 300,000 miles on that car."

This is longtime hotel employee Elmer Ashley, pictured at the Mason's front desk. His wife, Zelda, was a popular second-grade teacher in the Claremore public school system for many years.

Noted Oklahoma artist Charles Banks Wilson painted two scenes of the Mason Hotel's first and second floor lobby during the mid-1950s. The man in the chair examining the arrowhead collection is J.M. Davis. In 1970, Wilson would paint a portrait of Davis that still greets visitors to the Davis museum.

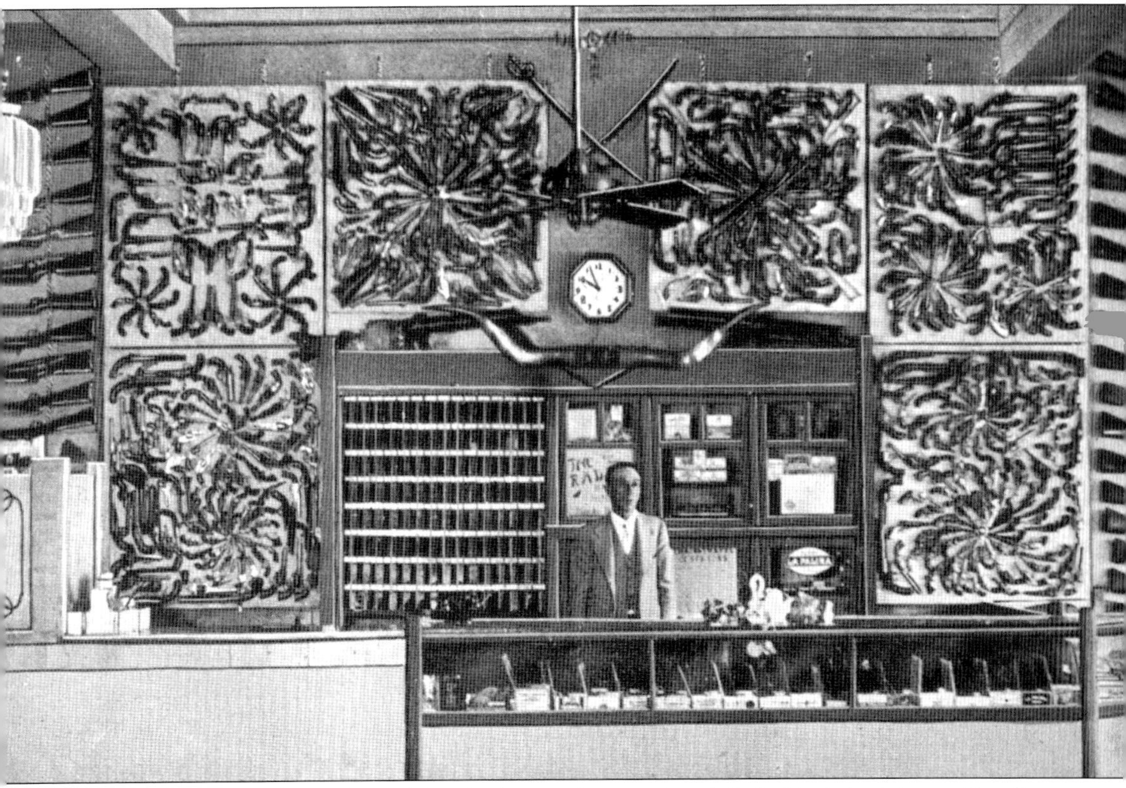

For many years, J.M. Davis himself worked a regular evening shift behind the Mason Hotel's registration desk. He took care of hotel business there, of course, checking a steady parade of guests in and out of rooms; but if one of them wanted to ask him about the unusual collection that took up the walls and other areas of the hotel, Davis was usually more than ready to chat.

In addition to the hotel lobby, the walls of the hotel's second floor were filled with weapons. Mounted longhorns of cattle and oxen jutted out from above each guestroom, and many of the bedroom walls were also lined with guns and related memorabilia.

One of the most interesting items displayed in the hotel was a Gatling gun, which greeted visitors from its place just inside the front door. Davis's collection featured many other pieces of Civil War vintage, including a cannon unearthed by a farmer near Fort Smith, Arkansas. Thinking he'd simply plowed up a big piece of rusted iron, the farmer was surprised to find it was a weapon used to defend Fort Smith during the war. Knowing of Davis and his collection, the farmer sent the cannon to Claremore as a gift.

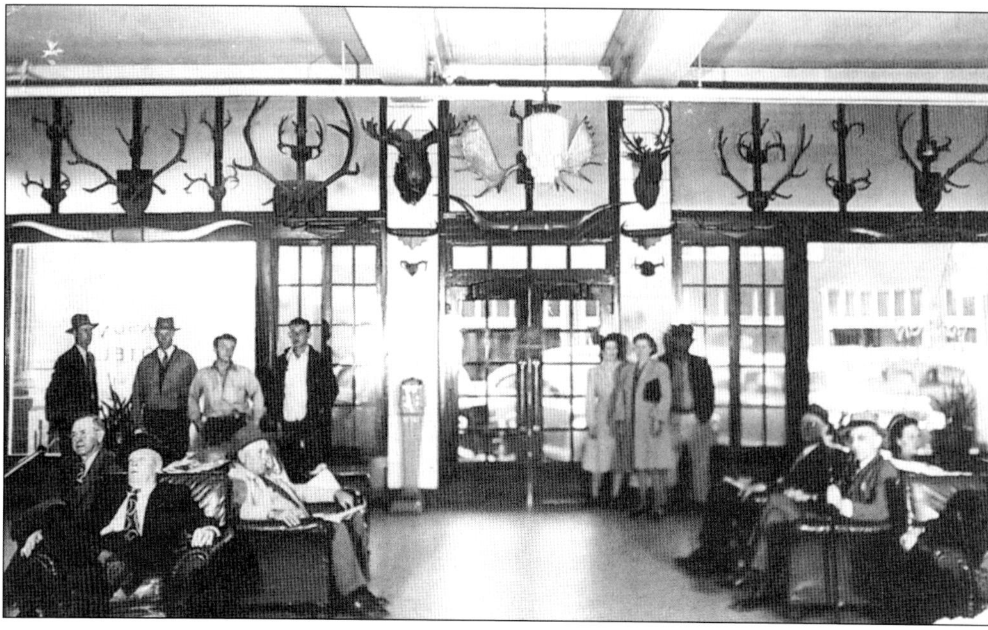

The lobby of the Mason Hotel stayed busy. In this 1940s photograph, hotel guests and town residents congregate just inside the front door, waiting to be seated in the coffee shop. The photograph below shows longtime Claremore banker Harry Hoagland making a purchase at the front desk counter.

Davis was a true gunsmith. His knowledge of arms went beyond knowing the caliber and manufacturer of each piece he owned. He also repaired and cleaned his treasures on a regular basis. In this 1946 photograph, Davis cleans one of the rifles in a collection that had grown, by that time, to more than 8,000 weapons and related memorabilia.

In 1956, the Oklahoma City Chamber of Commerce announced its interest in the J.M. Davis collection, with the idea that it could be housed in Oklahoma City's new Cowboy Hall of Fame. In a front-page *Claremore Progress* column, publisher Ed Livermore took the Oklahoma City Chamber to task, accusing the group of trying to strip small Oklahoma cities of their historical memories. Soon, newspapers across Oklahoma were taking sides about whether to move the Davis collection or keep it in Claremore. A new museum was still more than a decade away, but the fervor caused Claremore officials to take a beginning step. A three-man committee was appointed by Dorset Hacker, president of the Claremore Chamber of Commerce. That first Davis museum committee included A.M. Huffman, a real estate dealer; Harry Hoagland, vice-president of the First National Bank of Claremore; and Frank Podpechan, operator of the Rogers Coal Company.

When the Great Depression hit in the late 1920s, Addie Davis put her husband on a strict budget for his collecting, limiting him to an outlay of only $2,000 a month. That kind of money still bought a lot of weaponry, and Davis began to worry more and more about theft and destruction of his irreplaceable collection. Especially worrisome to him was the thought of a massive fire in the hotel. As early as the 1930s, he began contemplating the idea of a museum, but first the Depression and then World War II sidetracked his plans. When the museum finally became a reality, it wasn't a second too soon; during the hotel's final years, Davis hadn't been able to find an insurance company that would cover his possessions.

As the 1950s began, Addie's health started a slow decline, so she and J.M. decided to give up the day-to-day operation of the Mason Hotel Coffee Shop. Local businessman Bill Bailey was the first person to step in and operate the popular Claremore gathering place.

J.M. Davis is pictured standing beside the archway that connected the coffee shop to the main lobby.

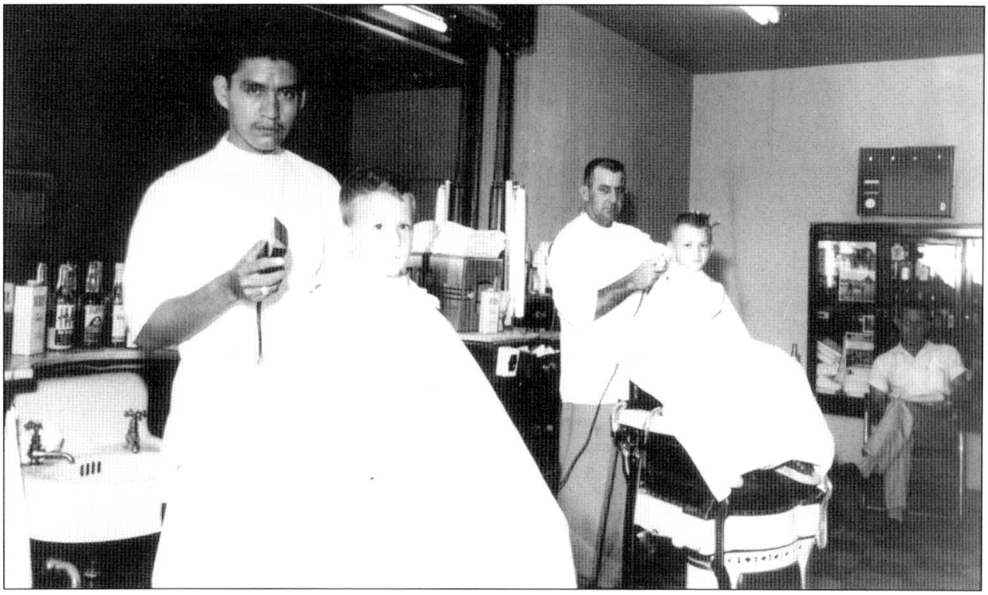

One of the various businesses in the Mason Hotel block was the barbershop of Foster Twist. He operated the haircutting shop from 1957 until his retirement in 1982. The shop was a popular location to hear the latest on local sports and politics. In the photograph, Twist (right) and longtime fellow barber Homer Panther lower the ears of a pair of youngsters.

Bob and Denyse Higgins, with their one-year-old son, Bill, would soon become neighbors to the barbershop. Denyse was a niece of Addie Davis. After Bob retired from the military, in 1958 the couple took over the operation of the coffee shop.

Even those who took a meal in the Mason Hotel's dining room could gaze upon collectors' items while enjoying their T-bones and chicken-fried steaks. In addition to its share of guns and other firearms, the dining room remained ringed with dozens of beer steins from around the world, a collecting passion shared by Davis and his wife.

To Bill Higgins and his younger sister Cathey, J.M. Davis and his wife were simply Uncle Monroe and Aunt Addie. "I was nine years old when we moved here, and even then I was in awe of them," Bill Higgins told the authors. "Both were special people and were always so nice. My parents ran the coffee shop at the Mason Hotel and Uncle Monroe allowed us to go about anywhere we wanted." Monroe was the name the Davis family and close friends used when talking about James Monroe Davis. Higgins remembered walking to the hotel from his home three blocks away. There in the coffee shop, he'd eat breakfast, read the daily paper, and walk to school.

After years of not much action and a lot of local disappointments, a deal was finally made to keep the J.M. Davis collection in Claremore. According to Donna McSpadden, her husband, Clem, who in 1965 was Oklahoma Senate President Pro Tem, invited Gov. Henry Bellmon to their home in Bushyhead. Bellmon and his entourage were touring northeastern Oklahoma, and McSpadden hoped to sit him down and work out a plan to endow the Davis collection to Oklahoma in return for the state's passing of the legislation necessary to fund a museum and foundation. If Bellmon approved, McSpadden would author the appropriate bill.

They were discussing the idea at the McSpadden home when Donna served chocolate cake to Bellmon and his party. As she told the authors, "the deal was made on a handshake and a piece of chocolate cake." Following the dessert and coffee, Bellmon and McSpadden drove straight to the Mason Hotel to seek Davis's approval. Hearing all the details, he was pleased and quickly agreed. His dream of a museum for his guns was about to come true. The McSpaddens were both involved in shaping and guiding the Davis Museum. Clem authored the bill to create the J.M. Davis Memorial and helped secure funding. Donna later served as chair on the Davis Memorial Commission.

Sadly, Mrs. Davis did not live to see the agreement and construction of the new museum. In 1959, a year before she and J.M. Davis would have celebrated their 50th wedding anniversary, Addie Lee Smith-Davis died after a short illness. She was laid to rest in Claremore's Woodland Cemetery under the direction of the Musgrove Funeral Home, now Musgrove-Merritt-Smith Funeral Service. She "just wore out," her doctors said. Rev. L.C. Robbins, pastor of First Baptist Church, said, "She had been a mother to the entire town. She will be missed by all." Addie was a longtime member of First Baptist. This is what the church looked liked during her years of membership.

Three

From Hotel Walls to Museum Halls 1966–1973

As the J.M. Davis Gun Museum booklet from the 1970s put it, "Mr. Davis continued to collect, the lobby walls became full, the Ballroom was filled to capacity! The walls of the long hall upstairs were lined everywhere you could see, and seven private rooms in the Hotel became full."

Clearly, the Davis collection had outgrown even the considerable dimensions of the Mason Hotel. In 1959, when Davis was 72 years old, his wife died. Addie had been a help and encouragement to Davis and his collecting from the beginning. According to Kathryn Clausen's book *A Portrait of Addie*, many who were close to the couple said she'd been even more than that, putting some of her own money into the collection and even purchasing some of the ancillary items herself. The couple had no children, and two years after Addie's passing, Davis married Genevieve Breeden, who was 20 years his junior.

By that time, informal talks had been going on for years regarding a museum to house the Davis collection. Finally, in the spring of 1965, the J.M. Davis Foundation was formed with Davis's wife Genevieve and nephew Dr. William R. Murphy as trustees. The Foundation then leased the collection to the State of Oklahoma for 99 years with the option to renew. That same year, the Oklahoma Legislature created the J.M. Davis Memorial Commission, whose first job was to find a suitable site and then purchase it with funds appropriated by the legislature.

The process took a while, but in 1967, the commission secured an area only a few blocks from the Mason Hotel. After much more work and deliberation, the museum opened two years later, on June 27, 1969, Davis's 82nd birthday. "Appropriate to the dedication," wrote Lauren Steele in the Tulsa Tribune, "Davis exploded the ceremonial ribbon with gun powder instead of cutting it."

Davis died in 1973, after the second phase of the museum was completed. Upon his death, about 12,000 pieces of his collection were being displayed there.

Two years after Addie's 1959 death, Davis married Genevieve Breeden. They had met years earlier while Davis was serving as mayor of Claremore and Genevieve was a secretary at city hall. Born near Claremore a year before Oklahoma's statehood, Genevieve was a Claremore High School graduate and one of 13 children born to Joseph Hayden Breeden and the former Martha Jane Swim, both Cherokee Indians. Married on July 21, 1961, at the Mayes County Courthouse, J.M. and Genevieve moved into the Mason Hotel, where he and Addie had made their home for years. Later in the decade, Genevieve assisted with the transfer of artifacts to the new Davis Museum. After Davis's death in 1973, she took over operation of the hotel and continued to run it until its 1980 closing. She passed away in 1997 and is entombed with her husband at the Davis Arms and Historical Museum. This photograph is from 1942

In this 1965 photograph, Oklahoma governor Henry Bellmon shakes hands with Genevieve Davis at the Mason Hotel shortly after "the largest private gun collection in the world" was leased to the State of Oklahoma. In return, the state was to construct a fireproof building to house the multimillion-dollar trove of antique and unusual firearms and other items. An earlier handshake between Governor Bellmon and J.M. Davis had sealed the deal for the funding and building of the museum.

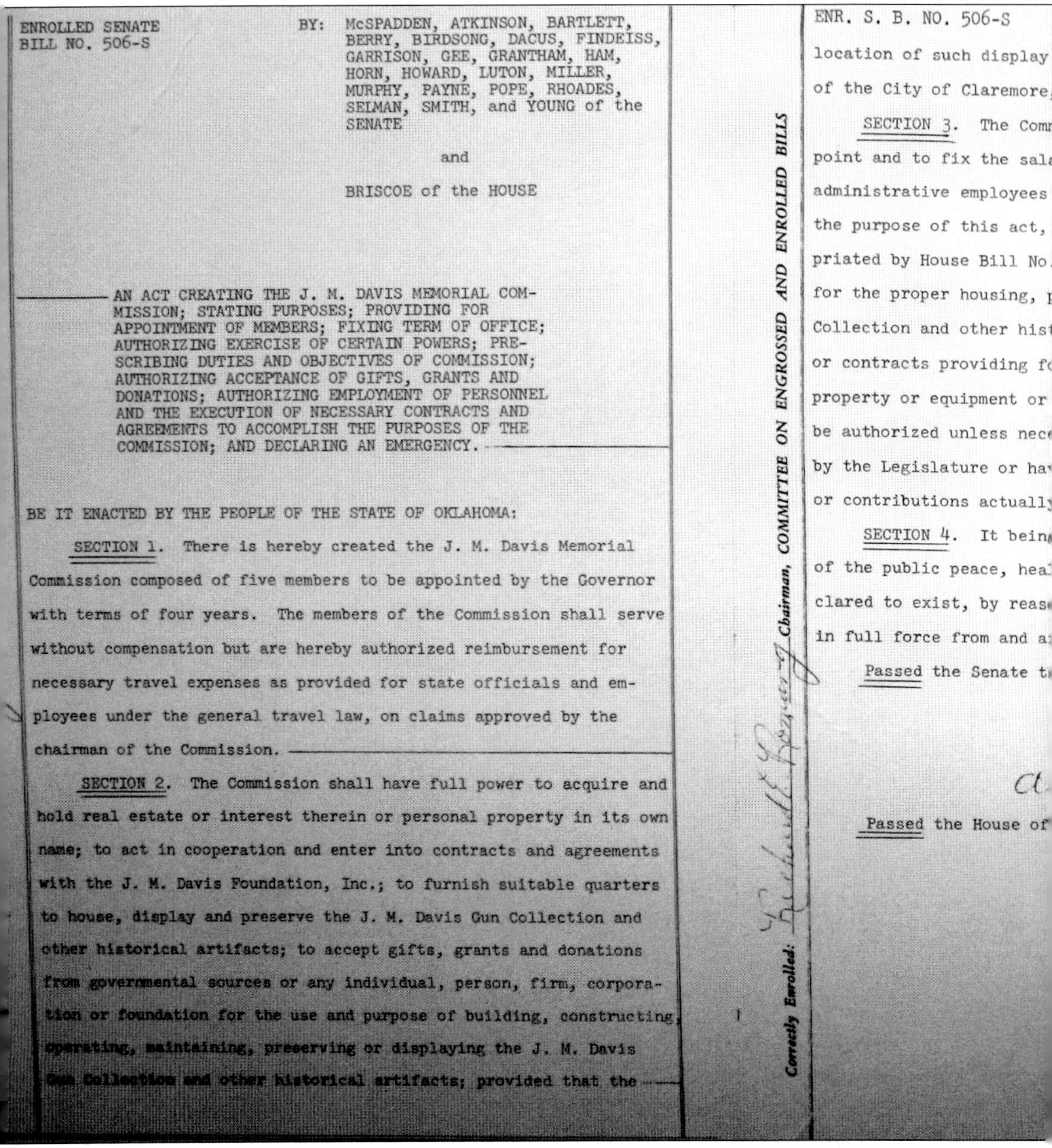
ENROLLED SENATE
BILL NO. 506-S

BY: McSPADDEN, ATKINSON, BARTLETT, BERRY, BIRDSONG, DACUS, FINDEISS, GARRISON, GEE, GRANTHAM, HAM, HORN, HOWARD, LUTON, MILLER, MURPHY, PAYNE, POPE, RHOADES, SELMAN, SMITH, and YOUNG of the SENATE

and

BRISCOE of the HOUSE

AN ACT CREATING THE J. M. DAVIS MEMORIAL COMMISSION; STATING PURPOSES; PROVIDING FOR APPOINTMENT OF MEMBERS; FIXING TERM OF OFFICE; AUTHORIZING EXERCISE OF CERTAIN POWERS; PRESCRIBING DUTIES AND OBJECTIVES OF COMMISSION; AUTHORIZING ACCEPTANCE OF GIFTS, GRANTS AND DONATIONS; AUTHORIZING EMPLOYMENT OF PERSONNEL AND THE EXECUTION OF NECESSARY CONTRACTS AND AGREEMENTS TO ACCOMPLISH THE PURPOSES OF THE COMMISSION; AND DECLARING AN EMERGENCY.

BE IT ENACTED BY THE PEOPLE OF THE STATE OF OKLAHOMA:

SECTION 1. There is hereby created the J. M. Davis Memorial Commission composed of five members to be appointed by the Governor with terms of four years. The members of the Commission shall serve without compensation but are hereby authorized reimbursement for necessary travel expenses as provided for state officials and employees under the general travel law, on claims approved by the chairman of the Commission.

SECTION 2. The Commission shall have full power to acquire and hold real estate or interest therein or personal property in its own name; to act in cooperation and enter into contracts and agreements with the J. M. Davis Foundation, Inc.; to furnish suitable quarters to house, display and preserve the J. M. Davis Gun Collection and other historical artifacts; to accept gifts, grants and donations from governmental sources or any individual, person, firm, corporation or foundation for the use and purpose of building, constructing, operating, maintaining, preserving or displaying the J. M. Davis Gun Collection and other historical artifacts; provided that the

Correctly Enrolled: [signature] Chairman, COMMITTEE ON ENGROSSED AND ENROLLED BILLS

ENR. S. B. NO. 506-S

location of such display
of the City of Claremore,

SECTION 3. The Comm
point and to fix the sala
administrative employees
the purpose of this act,
priated by House Bill No.
for the proper housing,
Collection and other his
or contracts providing f
property or equipment or
be authorized unless nec
by the Legislature or ha
or contributions actuall

SECTION 4. It bein
of the public peace, hea
clared to exist, by reas
in full force from and a

Passed the Senate t

Passed the House of

Shown is the original bill, authored by Oklahoma's Sen. Clem McSpadden, which created the J.M. Davis Memorial Commission. Received by Governor Bellmon at 2:15 p.m. on July 16, 1965,

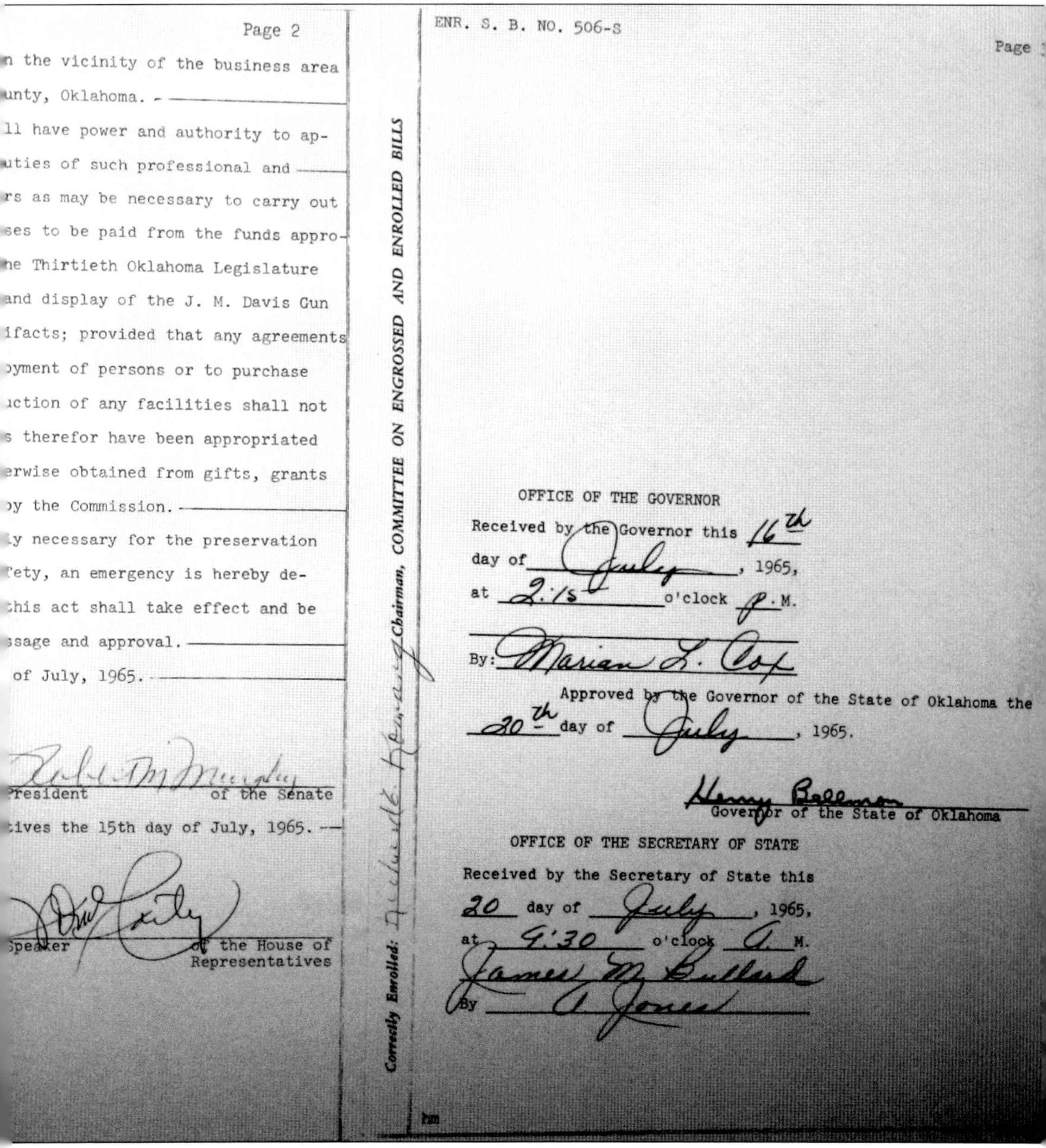
Page 2

n the vicinity of the business area
unty, Oklahoma.
ll have power and authority to ap-
uties of such professional and
rs as may be necessary to carry out
ses to be paid from the funds appro-
he Thirtieth Oklahoma Legislature
and display of the J. M. Davis Gun
ifacts; provided that any agreements
oyment of persons or to purchase
uction of any facilities shall not
s therefor have been appropriated
erwise obtained from gifts, grants
by the Commission.
ly necessary for the preservation
fety, an emergency is hereby de-
this act shall take effect and be
ssage and approval.
of July, 1965.

President of the Senate

tives the 15th day of July, 1965.

Speaker of the House of Representatives

Correctly Enrolled: Chairman, COMMITTEE ON ENGROSSED AND ENROLLED BILLS

ENR. S. B. NO. 506-S

Page

OFFICE OF THE GOVERNOR

Received by the Governor this 16th day of July, 1965, at 2:15 o'clock P.M.

By: Marian L. Cox

Approved by the Governor of the State of Oklahoma the 20th day of July, 1965.

Henry Bellmon
Governor of the State of Oklahoma

OFFICE OF THE SECRETARY OF STATE

Received by the Secretary of State this 20 day of July, 1965, at 9:30 o'clock A. M.

James M. Bullard
By A Jones

hm

it was approved and signed into law four days later.

Early in the process that eventually led to the building of the museum, members of the J.M. Davis Commission spent much of their time together poring over city maps and discussing the pros and cons of the five different sites then being considered as the permanent location for the Davis Museum. Members from left to right are Davis G. Murray, Tulsa architect and planner; chairman W.R. Kelley; and board members General J.F. Smoller, A.M. Huffman, C.H. March, and Wayne Rowley.

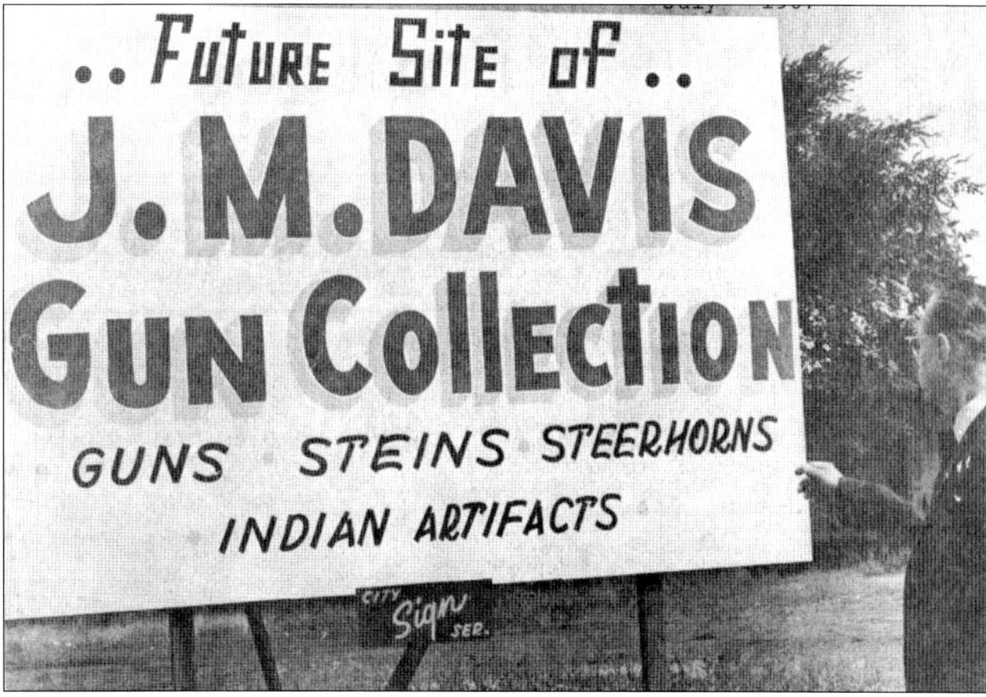

Rolland Kelley, chairman of the J.M. Davis Memorial Commission, looks at the new sign erected at the future site of the museum in this 1967 photograph. The area chosen was two blocks north of the Mason Hotel at what is now 330 North J.M. Davis Boulevard. The famed Main Street of America, Highway 66, ran to the immediate east and west of the property.

Bennie Garren (left), named first executive director of the J.M. Davis Museum, and Rolland Kelley, chairman of the Davis Commission, hold an original painting by Oklahoma artist Charles Banks Wilson. The painting was a gift to the commission from the Ford Motor Company, which had commissioned it to illustrate an article on the Davis collection that appeared in Ford's house publication, the *Ford Times*.

On a frigid Oklahoma day in January 1968, two blocks north of the Mason Hotel, J.M. and Genevieve Davis showed up to turn the first spades of earth in a ground-breaking ceremony for his future museum. Also on hand to help was the Davis' great-nephew David Taylor. Seen in the background is commission chairman Rolland Kelley and Oklahoma state senator Clem McSpadden.

A few weeks after the ground breaking, dirt was piling up in earnest as the first steps toward the brand-new museum continued. This photograph was taken on February 16, 1968.

A Hannaford Construction Company worker makes final preparations before pouring concrete and placing precast slabs at the future site of the J.M. Davis Gun Museum. The March 1968 photograph shows by that time, onlookers could begin to get a sense of the final size and shape of the building.

Like many Claremore youngsters in the 1950s and 1960s, Mickey Perry had fond memories of visiting J.M. Davis and his collection at the Mason Hotel. "All us boys enjoyed seeing the guns collected by Mr. Davis," he recalled. "I guess I was around 10 or 11 when I was first able to go there by myself. As long as we behaved ourselves, he didn't mind us. Fact is, I believe Mr. Davis was pleased that we would come around and admire his guns." Even in 1968, after the then-22-year-old Perry joined the Claremore Police Department, he continued his trips to see Davis at his establishment. "As a Claremore police patrolman, I always enjoyed stopping at the Mason Hotel to visit Davis. He was never too busy to talk about his collection, and he always had a new gun he wanted to show me." Perry went on to work for the Oklahoma State Narcotics Bureau before returning to Claremore, where he served as chief of police for 12 years. In all, Perry spent 41 years in law enforcement. Elected mayor of Claremore in 2011, he was inducted into the Oklahoma Law Enforcement Hall of Fame on December 14, 2013. Perry died unexpectedly two days later.

Here is the menu from the Mason Hotel and list of items. Always a popular place to eat, the Mason Hotel Coffee Shop was known for good food at moderate prices. Over 85 items were on the menu, with the most expensive being a $ 3.25 large T-bone steak served with salad, potatoes, and garlic toast. Also available were chicken and seafood dinners along with cold plates and hot sandwiches. There was also a breakfast menu. A large hot cup of coffee was only 10¢.

Even though passenger trains were largely a thing of the past, and most of the mineral-bath houses had closed by 1966 (when this photograph was taken), the Mason Hotel was still going strong, as evidenced by the dearth of empty parking spaces in front. The place remained a popular site for both tourists and locals who were drawn by J.M Davis's famed collection as well as the coffee shop and its diverse and reasonably priced menu items.

In 1968, less than a year before the first phase of the J.M. Davis museum opened, a man named C.C. Long opened his Long's Historical Museum just down the hill a few blocks from Claremore's Will Rogers Memorial. Advertised as containing "over 50,000 items of historical importance from all over the world, dating back to the 17th century," its primary attractions for many years were its wax figures of people ranging from Attila the Hun and Jesus and his disciples at the Last Supper to the Beatles, Elvis, and Frank Sinatra. There was even a waxen effigy of Long himself. Unlike the Davis collection, the Longs Historical Museum did not stay in Claremore after its founder's death. According to April Churchill and Dorothy Kizer-Dennis, authors of the book *Claremore* (Arcadia Publishing, 2007), his son Jack moved the museum to Florida sometime in the late 1970s. Today, a Reasor's food store is located on the former Long's location, 1000 West Will Rogers Boulevard.

OFFICIAL PUBLIC OPENING

J. M. Davis Gun Museum

CLAREMORE, OKLAHOMA

June 27, 1969

1:30 P.M.

Here is the program cover for museum dedication day. All of the hundreds who attended the official opening of the J.M. Davis Gun Museum on June 27, 1969, received one of these programs. The event began with the Presentation of Colors and the Pledge of Allegiance, led by American Legion Post No. 141. The Claremore Civic Symphonic Band followed with "The Star Spangled Banner."

RIBBON CUTTING CEREMONY

Senator Clem McSpadden - - Master of Ceremonies

☆

PROGRAM

Presentation of Colors - American Legion Post No. 141

Pledge of Allegiance - American Legion Post No. 141

Star Spangled Banner - Claremore Civic Symphonic Band

Invocation - - - The Reverend Mr. O. C. Wickstrom
First Christian Church, Claremore

Introduction of Guests - - Senator Clem McSpadden

Inception of the J. M. Davis Gun Museum - - - U. S. Senator Henry Bellmon

Impact on Tourism - - - Governor Dewey Bartlett

Expression of Appreciation - - Jack Marshall, Mayor

Presentation - - - - - W. R. Kelley, Chairman
J. M. Davis Memorial Commission

Gun Salute to Mr. Davis - - - V. F. W. Post No. 2976

Cutting of the Ribbon - - - - - Mr. J. M. Davis

Shown is a look inside the program for the day's events. Mayor Jack Marshall expressed the city's appreciation, and W.R. Kelley, chairman of the J.M. Davis Memorial Commission, made the presentation. Just before the ribbon cutting, V.F.W. Post 2976 honored Davis with a gun salute. Former governor Henry Bellmon, now a US senator, and his successor, Governor Dewey Bartlett, then looked on as Davis cut the ribbon across the front doors. Oklahoma state senator Clem McSpadden served as master of ceremonies.

Pictured is the official portrait of J.M. Davis commissioned for the Davis Museum. Famed Oklahoma artist Charles Banks Wilson painted this portrait of J.M. Davis in his familiar position behind the registration desk at the Mason Hotel. According to writer Patt Cameron, "Wilson said the portrait had been a real challenge for him because Davis could only hold a pose for 10 to 15 minutes at a time."

Charles Banks Wilson, a resident of Miami, was already well known as a painter and illustrator at the time, and one of his works was already hanging in the museum (see page 71). He was the unanimous choice by area friends and supporters to do the painting. Among them, they raised $3,000 to commission Wilson, whose work had been displayed in such noteworthy places as the New York Metropolitan Museum, the Library of Congress in Washington, DC, and Oklahoma's State Capitol building. Wilson's portrait of Davis was officially unveiled during the open house at the museum on March 5, 1970. Note the detail on the gun exhibit in the background. This painting can currently be viewed as a part of the replica of the Mason Hotel lobby display in the Davis Museum.

A decades-long fear of J.M. Davis's nearly became reality on February 20, 1970, when a fire broke out directly across the street from the hotel in Copp's Café. During a busy lunch hour, grease had spilled over into the flames and ignited. The stove was covered with steaks and hamburgers, and the exhaust fans sucked the flames up to the ceiling, where they rapidly spread. Before the fire could be extinguished by firefighters from Collinsville and Pryor along with the men of the Claremore Fire Department, half the block of 600 West Will Rogers was completely destroyed; black boiling smoke could be seen for miles. When it was all over, damages were estimated at a $250,000, with the dentist office of Dr. Jim Marshall one of the most prominent buildings consumed by the flames. After years of standing vacant, the ravaged block has become home to a Walgreen Drug Store on the east side and Claremore Tire on the west. Although this photograph was taken about 15 years before the fire, one can see how close the flames were to the Mason Hotel. Copp's Café is on the extreme right of this photograph by the Coca-Cola sign. While the firemen battled the flames, Davis could be seen on the roof of the Mason Hotel with water buckets.

Sue Cook (left) and Shirley Johnson (right) were two early museum employees who helped catalog, transfer, and display Davis's collectibles. In this photograph from the spring of 1969, the two ladies look through his extensive collection of John Rogers statuary. Both women would go on to become executive directors of the museum. Cook served in that capacity from 1974 to 1989, and Johnson from 1998 to 2001.

The first executive secretary of the Davis Museum was Pearl Golden from 1967 to 1970. Named executive director in 1970, she oversaw the two building expansions during her four years as director. Her husband, Russell, was retired from the Oklahoma Military Academy and operated several businesses in Claremore. Pearl also owned and operated the Will Rogers Hotel and Coffee Shop in the 1980s and 1990s.

Cy Vogt was a well-known and well-liked area farmer and businessman who operated a large turkey farm near Claremore Lake for many years. In the 1960s, he went to work for J.M. Davis as a research specialist, cataloguing items as they were transferred from the Mason Hotel to the new Davis Museum, as well as repairing many pieces in the John Rogers statuary and stein collection. Known for his attention to detail, Vogt became the museum's first curator, retiring from that position in the mid-1980s.

From the beginning, the Davis Memorial Commission has overseen the museum's operation. In June 1972, its members included, from left to right, C.H. March, chairman A.M. Huffman, and Rolland Kelley.

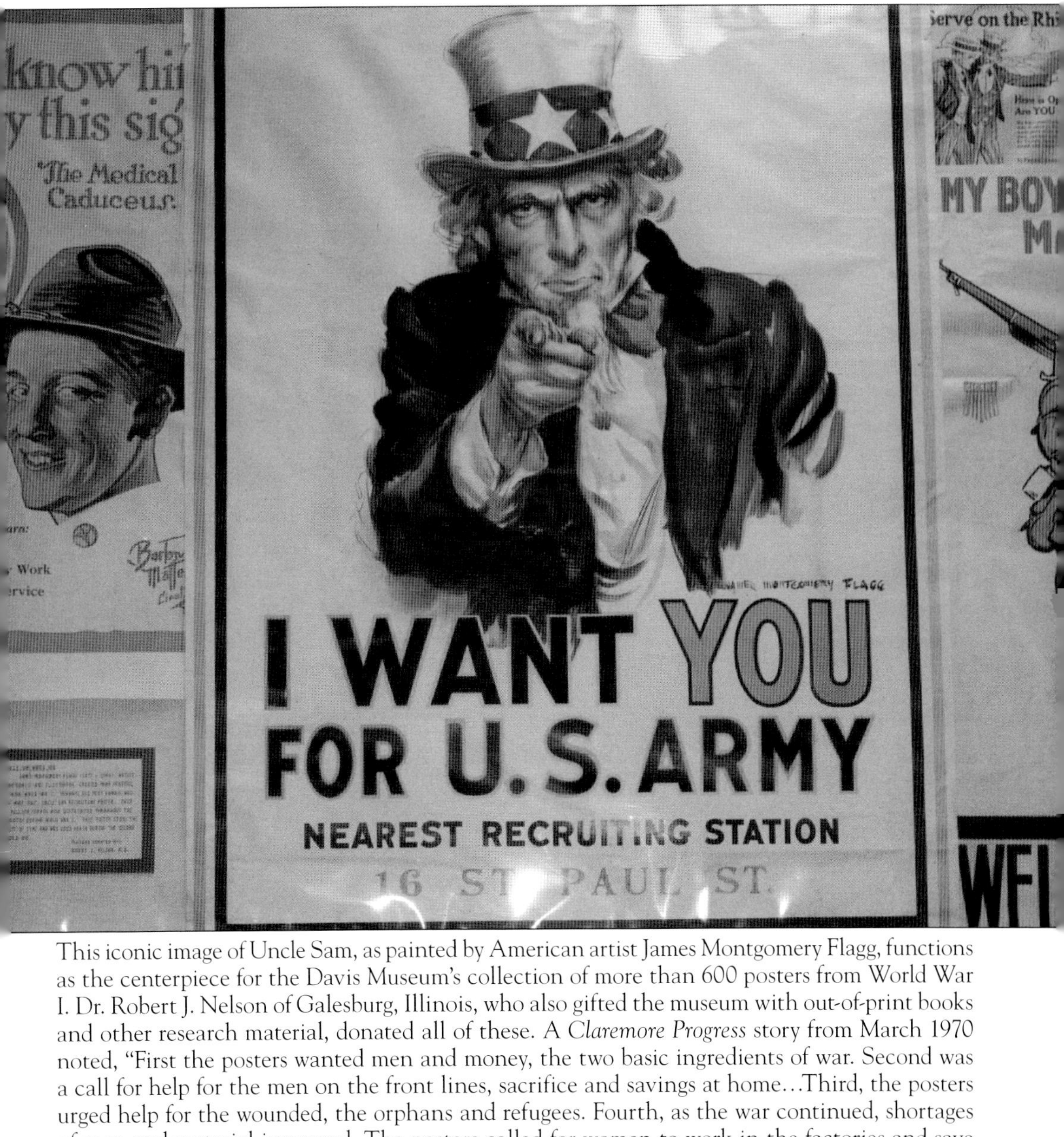

This iconic image of Uncle Sam, as painted by American artist James Montgomery Flagg, functions as the centerpiece for the Davis Museum's collection of more than 600 posters from World War I. Dr. Robert J. Nelson of Galesburg, Illinois, who also gifted the museum with out-of-print books and other research material, donated all of these. A *Claremore Progress* story from March 1970 noted, "First the posters wanted men and money, the two basic ingredients of war. Second was a call for help for the men on the front lines, sacrifice and savings at home…Third, the posters urged help for the wounded, the orphans and refugees. Fourth, as the war continued, shortages of men and material increased. The posters called for women to work in the factories and save vital materials for the war effort." Each of these themes is forcefully presented in the posters on display at the museum.

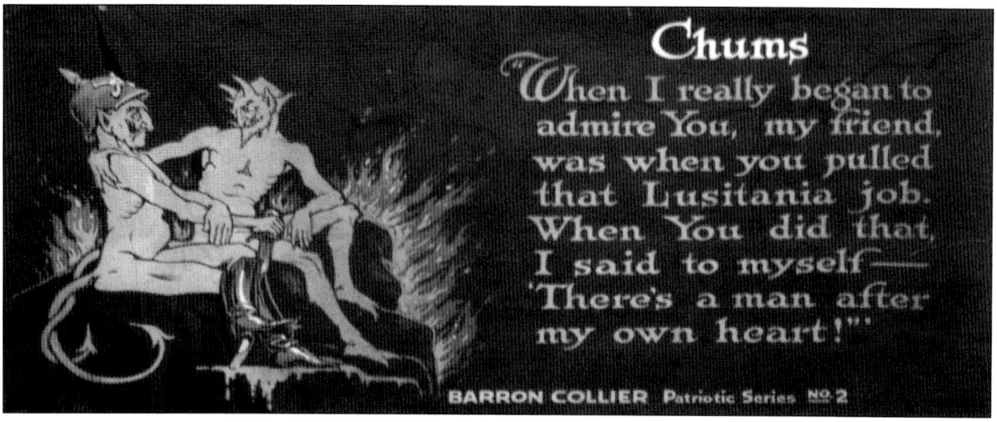

Viewed today, some of the World War I posters now hanging in the J.M. Davis Museum seem extreme and even unsettling, especially a series that equates German Emperor Kaiser Wilhelm II with Satan himself. America had been plunged into the "War to End All Wars," the gloves were off, and lurid posters were a quick and effective way to sum up viciousness of the enemy.

As his weaponry and other elements of his collection were being transferred to their new home, Davis was a frequent visitor to the building two blocks north of the Mason Hotel. He enjoyed exploring the place and looking over potential sites for different displays.

Decades before the first spade of dirt was turned on the lot that would become his museum, J.M. Davis had begun dreaming about a permanent home for his collection. Now, it had become a reality.

The J.M. Davis Arms and Historical Museum was built in three phases. The first opened in June 1969, and the second in June 1972. Oklahoma state senator Bob Wadley served as master of ceremonies for the 1972 opening.

J.M. and Genevieve Davis are welcomed as they arrive for the 1972 ceremonies. Immediately to their right are Mr. and Mrs. W.R. Kelley of the Davis Memorial Commission. Behind them are Claremore business owners Mr. and Mrs. Phil Smith.

Once he was seated, Mr. Davis felt right at home, hefting a pistol in one hand and a rifle in the other. Behind him in this photograph are Claremore mayor Kiefer Curlee and his wife.

On Jan. 20, 1973, J.M. Davis was walking down the stairs of the Mason Hotel when he missed the last step, stumbled, and hit the lobby floor on his head. Rushed to the Claremore Health Center with a head injury, he drifted in and out of consciousness before passing away on Feb. 7. The body lay in state on February 8 and 9 and then was moved to the First Christian Church for a Saturday afternoon service, with Rev. O.C. Wickstrom officiating. He was laid to rest in Claremore's Woodlawn Cemetery, where his first wife, Addie, was buried. In addition to becoming famous well beyond his city for his superlative collection, Davis had lived a long, successful life as a businessman and local political figure, owning and operating the Mason Hotel for 43 years, serving six terms as Claremore's mayor, and receiving the chamber of commerce's 1967 Man of the Year award. In recognition of his stature, the mayor declared Claremore to be in an official state of mourning for three days. On January 9, 1974, a public hearing was held regarding the J.M. Davis Memorial Commission's application for a permit to entomb Mr. Davis and, following her death, Genevieve Davis, within the museum's walls. The permit was approved. After Genevieve Davis's passing in 1997, she was reunited with her husband at the museum. Along with Will Rogers and his immediate family, who are buried beneath the Will Rogers Memorial Museum in Claremore, J.M. and Genevieve Davis are the only people buried on property belonging to the State of Oklahoma.

Four

A Collection for the Ages

1974 and Beyond

"If a student of history and gun lore goes to the J.M. Davis Gun Museum every week for the next 10 years," wrote June Harms in the September 5, 1969, *Tulsa Tribune*, "he'll see something new every time."

The statement was true then, and it is even truer today. In the nearly 50 years since Davis's death, the museum—whose name was changed in 1994 to reflect the increasing diversity of the items on display—does not only delight thousands of visitors a year with the firearms and other collectibles amassed by J.M. Davis himself, but it also honors his legacy and passion by keeping things fresh with new acquisitions.

For instance, said curator Jason Schubert, "The commission purchased a full-scale replica of a three-inch Parrott gun [used in the Civil War] that we have here with a carriage and limber—the box that holds the ammo—with mannequins of a uniformed rider and the horses pulling the carriage. We've also had several donations of historic Rogers County lawmen's guns, which date back to pre-statehood. And we have exhibits from the first Gulf War as well."

And that just scratches the surface. Hardly a week goes by when the museum is not contacted about another possible addition to this vastly impressive collection of exhibits.

Of course, it could not continue to prosper without help, which comes from a wide variety of sources. In 2015, for instance, the State of Oklahoma invested $346,000 in the museum, financing a new roof, new entrance doors, and other mechanical upgrades. The next year, Pelco Structural of Claremore donated equipment for a video display of the members of the Claremore Hall of Fame, Rogers County residents who have not only made a difference in northeastern Oklahoma, but also statewide, nationally, and even internationally. And, three years after that, a generous grant from the Grand River Dam Authority brought a complete LED outdoor-lighting upgrade. The Friends of the Museum have also continued their invaluable support, raising funds for such things as parking lot sealing and new benches for the Mason Hotel lobby display.

So, the legacy that began when the father of a sickly child finally enticed him to take his medicine by offering the bribe of a shotgun grows with each passing year. The Mason Hotel may have long ago fallen to the wrecking ball, but J.M. Davis's "greatest collection of guns in the world" lives on, more than ready for its next half-century of wowing visitors from all over. As one of the top attractions along America's iconic Route 66, the J.M. Davis Arms & Historical Museum not only continues to house the world's largest privately held arms collection, but it also shines a bright light into the past, illuminating Oklahoma's rich Native American and Western heritage for all to experience.

In 1979, Lee Trimble Good was profiled in *OK* magazine, a Sunday supplement published by the *Tulsa World* newspaper. One could call Lee Good "the Gunfather." The first director of the J.M. Davis Arms and Historical Museum, he remained in that position until his November 1998 death. A graduate of Will Rogers High School in Tulsa, Good had a long fascination with black-powder weaponry. This led to his first visit to Claremore and the Mason Hotel. Told that countless weapons, including black-powder guns, were hanging on the walls, Good had to see them. Little did he realize the connection he'd have years later with those guns. Following a tour in the US Navy, Good attended Tulsa University and helped his father in the dry-cleaning business. Weapons remained his passion, and when the time came for the massive Davis collection to be transferred from the Mason Hotel to the newly built museum, Good was the man for the job—and a huge job it was. Thousands of weapons and other memorabilia lined the walls of Davis's hotel, but just as many, if not more, were stacked up in various rooms throughout the building. "It was mind-boggling as we continued to find an amazing assortment of firearms from all over the world," Good later said.

Some two months before the official opening of what then the J.M. Davis Gun Museum, Lee Good was on the scene as a research assistant. That began a long association with the museum that saw him become executive director and curator, overseeing its growth into the international tourist attraction that it has become. Although Good was an expert on all sorts of firearms, he was particularly knowledgeable about the history of black powder guns, writing a column on the subject for many years in a national magazine. His love of muzzle-loading firearms and other weapons was reflected in his service as director of the National Muzzle Loading Rifle Association and the founder and president of the Osage Territory Muzzle Loaders. He is also an inductee into the National Muzzle Loaders Hall of Fame. He passed away on November 20, 1998, while going about his duties in the museum.

The J.M. Davis Gun Museum opened on its namesake's 82nd birthday, June 27, 1969. For that opening, a medallion was struck in his honor. Produced by the Franklin Mint, it depicted Davis and his guns on the front and other items from his collection on the back. One hundred sterling silver medallions were made, with a limited number of others cast in bronze. The first medallion was presented to Davis at the opening. Three years later, on his 85th birthday, a Claremore street was named in his honor. The original Route 66 through Claremore, which ran just west of the museum, had been Wichita Street. Now, it was J.M. Davis Boulevard.

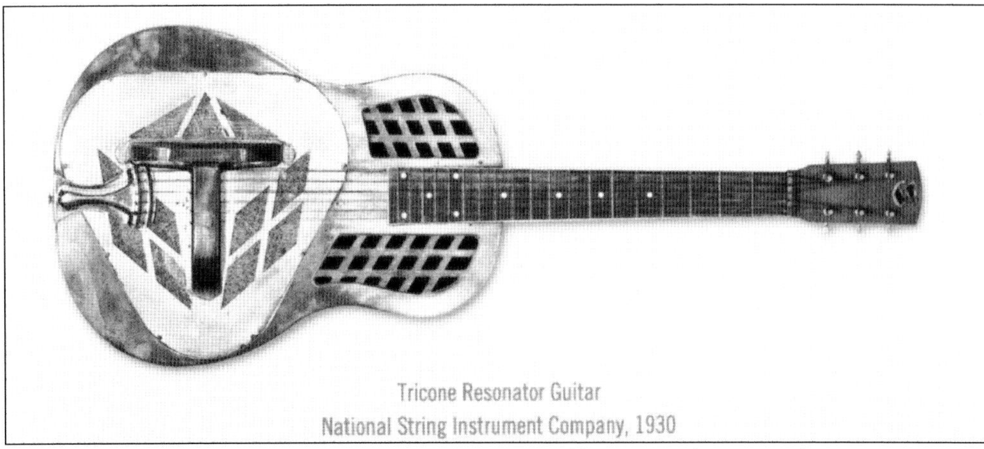

Among the many non-weapon artifacts in the Davis collection are his musical instruments. The museum displays dozens of violins and other stringed instruments, along with brass, woodwinds, and percussion. One unique item is a Gold-Tone National Tricone Resonator guitar. In the days before electronic amplifiers, guitars often got drowned out by the louder instruments in the band. George Beauchamp and John Dopyera created a single flattened resonating cone mechanism and placed it inside the guitar body, creating the Tricone Resonator guitar—a first step in bringing the guitar to the front as a solo instrument.

In June 2011, Jerry Wiley (right) and his wife, Sheila, of Shell Knob, Missouri, presented curator Jason Schubert and the Davis Museum with a gift that had been promised to J.M. Davis 67 years earlier. Capt. Robert McHolland, Wiley's uncle, had come across the 18th-century French pistol while serving in World War II. In 1944, McHolland wrote a Claremore cousin to tell Davis that he had "a very antique French pistol I'm saving for his collection of guns." Shortly after writing that letter, however, McHolland was killed in action in Germany. The pistol was eventually handed down to Wiley, who discovered the original letter much later. He then decided to donate the pistol to Davis's collection, making it (technically) the final firearm J.M. Davis acquired, 38 years after his death.

It was strictly a matter of starting at the bottom of the totem pole for Shirley Johnson and her 30-year career at the J.M. Davis Museum. She was only looking for a part-time job when she accepted a position at the museum in 1971. In 2001, she retired as executive director. Johnson was appointed to the position in 1998, following the death of Lee Good. Good had been in charge of moving the Davis collection from the Mason Hotel to the new facility. "Lee had a vision for the entire collection, but it was the guns that were special to him," said Johnson during a 2012 interview. "He pushed for quality instead of quantity. His knowledge of all types of firearms was remarkable. He wrote countless magazine articles on all kinds of guns." Following her husband's retirement, Shirley Johnson and her family moved to Claremore from Stillwater in 1970. It did not take long before she realized she needed something to keep her busy outside the home. Rose Walker, a good friend from church, recommended she seek employment at the museum. The collection was in the middle of being transferred, and workers were needed. "I started at the bottom," she recalled with a smile, "I worked in the gift shop, helped put up new displays, took inventory, arranged the steins, and recorded history—Anything that needed doing." When Good died, Johnson found herself next in line. "I didn't want the job, but with Lee suddenly gone it fell on my shoulders," she said, "All of us knew nobody could really replace him. I did accept the position for the next couple of years leading up to my retirement. By agreeing to do so, the Davis Commission board was not rushed into finding a solid replacement." Photographs of Shirley Johnson are found on pages 74 and 117 in this book.

Although the Mason ceased to function as a hotel in 1974, the ancient building struggled along for another dozen years, housing antique shops and other small businesses before finally succumbing to the wrecking ball in 1986. A caption in the May 23, 1986, *Claremore Progress* told the tale succinctly: "The boom was lowered Tuesday on the old Mason Hotel and the J.M. Davis collection home, drawing hundreds of straw bosses as workmen pounded away at the Claremore landmark. Brick by brick the facade fell away, leaving only the skeleton to be hauled away in dump trucks." And so ended the life of the 76-year-old Claremore landmark and its coffee shop, enjoyed by generations of visitors and hometown folk and famous for years as the home of its owner's fabulous firearms collection.

In this photograph, the second story of the Mason Hotel goes down to the wrecking ball.

In 1968, after director Arthur Penn's biopic *Bonnie and Clyde* had become a huge hit, visitors to the Mason Hotel wanted to see the outlaw duo's real-life pistols. That's according to *Kansas City Times* reporter John T. Alexander, who wrote a May 28, 1968, piece about Davis and his collection. In Alexander's telling, Davis couldn't quite remember where he had them displayed. The weapons aren't hard to find today, as they're part of the Gallery of Outlaw Guns exhibit, which features 30 firearms that once belonged to lawbreakers of all stripes. In addition to the Bonnie and Clyde weaponry, the popular display includes a pistol that once belonged to Depression-era gangster Charles "Pretty Boy" Floyd with a getaway map etched in its grip.

Henry Starr is the only well-known outlaw to have actually stayed overnight in the Mason Hotel. Several of his ilk, however, are represented in the J.M. Davis collection. Jesse James's Smith & Wesson has always attracted much attention. Other weapons were once owned by a range of colorful bandits including Alvin Barker, the Dalton brothers, and even Pancho Villa. In addition, a .41 Remington Derringer presented to Wild Bill Hickok is on display, along with an old Winchester rifle owned by Belle Starr at the time she was killed.

The Davis Museum and the Daisy Outdoor Products Company of Rogers, Arkansas, hosts an annual Daisy BB Gun Days. Company representatives bring an indoor shooting range to Claremore, which is set up inside the museum. On a Friday night, the museum hosts a celebrity and adult shooting contest along with silent and live auctions. On Saturday, kids aged 18 and under shoot for free for a chance to win a custom-made Daisy Red Ryder BB Rifle. Pictured from left to right are Joe Murfin, vice-president of marketing for Daisy Outdoor; Jim Dry, event chairman; and Daisy products expert and Davis Museum curator, Jason Schubert.

Winners of the 2011 Daisy BB Gun Days included Scott Shelton, 15, of Oologah, Oklahoma, who took first place in the senior youth division, scoring 25 out of 30 and winning the Daisy Red Ryder BB rifle.

Seven-year-old Adrian Tipton of Leesville, Louisiana, showed everyone how it was done in the 2011 contest, scoring 28 out of a possible 30. Here, museum curator Jason Schubert poses with Adrian and his prize.

One of the most unusual and unsettling collections in the museum is made up of weapons confiscated by the Claremore Police Department. Many are hand-crafted; all are deadly. In addition to pistols and sawed-off shotguns, the display includes homemade knives, baseball bat clubs, and brass knuckles. All of these items were taken by policemen during arrests and routine stops. Before being moved to the museum, this collection was housed at the Claremore Police Department, two blocks down the street from the Mason Hotel.

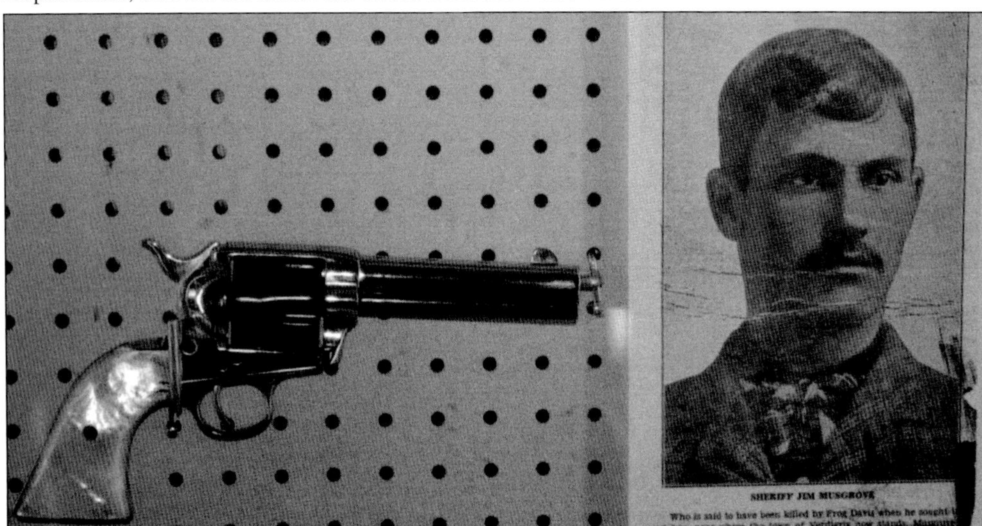

A long-running and popular display at the museum, this exhibit features weaponry from—and photographs of—law officers as far back as the Wild West days of pre-statehood Oklahoma. Chief among the artifacts from that era is a revolver that belonged to James T. Musgrove, a cousin of Will Rogers who was sheriff in 1895 of the Cooweescoowee District of the Cherokee Nation. The memorabilia also includes a gun that belonged to Tyrus R. Cobb, who was not the famed baseball player, but the first member of the Oklahoma Highway Patrol to come from Rogers County. Interestingly, he resided in the Mason Hotel. Another pioneering lawman represented in the display is Ronald Jackson, who, in February 1968, became the first African American Highway Patrolman. His service revolver and ID badge are among the many items donated by people from in and around Claremore.

In 2014, curator Jason Schubert designed a popular World War I exhibit. It includes dozens of war-related posters and artifacts, including helmets, weapons, mess kits, and knives. From left to right, Northeast Technology Center, Claremore, students Sam Brassfield, Mitch McCullough, and Blake Thomas created a World War I documentary film for the exhibit.

Since 2012, a group known as the Tri-State Gunfighters has entertained museum visitors with an event dubbed the High Noon Shoot Out. Outfitted in authentic 1870s-style garb and using replica weapons from the same decade, the Tri-State Gunfighters stage noontime shootouts, bank robberies, jailbreaks, and other exciting Old West reenactments, held on the first Saturday of the months of April through October. Hailing from Broken Arrow, Collinsville, Dewey, Owasso, Tulsa, and Claremore, these spirited men and women also represent the museum at parades and other events.

One of the Davis Museum's best-known exhibits stands outside the building itself, a landmark for years to motorists driving Oklahoma's Route 66. It is a US M41 Bulldog Walker light tank used by US forces in the Korean War and, later, by South Vietnamese army troops. It was first displayed at the museum in February 1988, and thousands of photographs have been taken of it since.

In the fall of 2012, the tank received a fresh coat of paint courtesy the US Army supplying the paint and Gerber Collision of Claremore supplying the manpower. A tent covered the tank during the work to prevent passing vehicles from getting "streaked" as the paint was applied.

When youngster Ray Akin III was delivering newspapers in downtown Claremore, the Mason Hotel was one of his final stops. He always saved a wrinkle-free paper for Davis, who waited for it behind the reception desk. The newspaper carrier would grow up and join his father in the plumbing business. He would also follow in the footsteps of J.M. Davis, serving on the Claremore City Council and also becoming mayor. At a Friends of the J.M. Davis Museum meeting, he told about going to the Mason Hotel in his younger days to deal with a plumbing problem. "I get there and Mr. Davis is behind the counter like always," Akin remembered. "He tells me what room to go to. I go up by myself, find the trouble, and quickly fix it. Like all the other upstairs rooms, this one was full of guns. As I'm gathering my tools I can see this gun barely sticking out of a box. What caused me to pick it up, I don't know. I do remember it being real nice. Just as I'm putting it back I hear Mr. Davis coming into the room. I was caught and I figured I was in big trouble; if not from Mr. Davis then from my dad, when he found out I had been snooping. Instead of being angry, Mr. Davis simply said the gun was a nice piece and how he obtained it. I don't know how he knew which weapon I was looking at since he didn't actually see me with it, but he knew just the same. Much to my relief," Akin concluded, "he never mentioned that day to my dad, either."

Most of the historical material displayed on the walls and in the cases that line the aisles of the J.M. Davis Museum has the power to fire the imagination, but perhaps no single exhibit does it better than its collection of kids' guns. While much of this juvenile weaponry is naturally associated with movie, radio, and television cowboys of a bygone era, such as Gene Autry, Roy Rogers, and the Lone Ranger, one of these pieces belongs with a space helmet instead of a ten-gallon hat. It's the Buck Rogers Disintegrator Pistol, first manufactured by the Daisy Manufacturing Company in the 1930s. By the time these pistols came out, the interplanetary character Buck Rogers had a huge youthful following from both a radio show and the successful newspaper comic, *Buck Rogers in the 25th Century*—America's first science-fiction comic strip.

Along with Oklahoma state senator Sean Burrage, Rep. Tad Jones (left) and Sen. Marty Quinn (right) were instrumental in obtaining $346,200 from the Oklahoma Legislature for capital improvements at the museum. Here, executive director Wayne McCombs thanks Jones and Quinn atop the museum's new roof, one of many improvements made possible by the funding.

California's Charles R. Suydam was internationally known as both an arms collector and expert writer on the subjects of cartridges and firearms. He was also a great friend of the J.M. Davis Museum and its executive director in the 1980s and 1990s, Lee Good. Over the years, Suydam not only visited the museum many times, but also donated his research library of some 1,300 books on weaponry and related topics. Because of his generosity, the library's reference collection was named the Charles R. Suydam Library on October 22, 1999. During his last visit to the museum, following Lee Good's passing, Suydam donated a silver-and-turquoise bolo tie as a token of the longtime friendship between the two men. It remains on display, a symbol of the generosity of one of the museum's most ardent supporters.

Here, the couple responsible for the world's largest gun show visits the greatest private collection of guns in the world and its curator, Jason Schubert (left). In 2011, Joe and Kathy Wanenmacher posed for this photograph with Schubert at the J.M. Davis Museum. Joe Wanenmacher is the originator and manager of the Tulsa Arms Show, a twice-yearly event that, like the museum, features miles of guns and other weaponry. Unlike the museum, the firearms at the Tulsa Arms Show are for sale at more than 4,100 dealers' tables. The Wanemacher events are held each spring and fall at the Quik Trip Center on the Tulsa Fairgrounds.

He was young and handsome. He was polite to all women and friendly with most men. He was charming and even appeared in an early Western movie titled *A Debtor to the Law*, drawn from his life story. Henry Starr was all this and more. Most notably, he was a bank robber. According to Oklahoma history buffs, this part-Cherokee bad boy may have robbed more financial institutions than any other outlaw in history. Considering the exploits of Jesse James, the Dalton brothers, and Bill Doolin's gang, that is an impressive bunch of hold-ups. Despite his bad habit of robbing banks, it was apparently hard to dislike Starr. He made friends everywhere he went. This included his one-year stay in Claremore in 1920, a year before his death. He rented a room at the Mason Hotel, where he met owner and gun collector J.M. Davis. By this time, Starr had been tried for murder and various other crimes, had spent time in prison in two different states, and had been pardoned by Pres. Theodore Roosevelt. He also had produced and starred in the above-mentioned feature film based on his bank-robbing career. During his Claremore stay, Starr was a model citizen—until one night in a local tavern. Apparently, an argument started between him and the bartender. While the full details are not clear, the incident led to Starr leaving town for good shortly afterwards. His father, George "Hop" Starr, was half Cherokee and a member of a family devoted to crime. Hop's brother was the infamous Sam Starr, husband of outlaw queen Belle Starr, but the worst of the bunch was their father, Tom Starr. A noted killer and thief, he was later called "the Devil's own" by his grandson. Henry's life of crime started at 16 with his arrest for bringing a wagonload of whiskey into Indian Territory. Five years later, he took a horse that did not belong to him. Bank robbing seemed to suit him the best, however. Once he started, he could not quit. "You walk into one, point a pistol, and they give you money," Starr once explained. During a gunfight with US deputy marshals in the summer of 1892, Starr killed a lawman named Floyd Wilson. A year later, Starr was caught in Colorado and returned to Fort Smith to stand trial for highway robbery and murder. He was sentenced to hang, but the conviction was overturned twice before he was ultimately convicted on the non-hanging offense of manslaughter. While in prison, Starr saved the life of a guard. This heroic action was key to his earning a pardon from President Roosevelt. Still, he could not stay out of banks. He was captured in Colorado a second time and put back behind bars, where he studied law and wrote his autobiography. The governor set him free when Starr promised not to leave the state. He did, however, and picked up where he had left off as a civilian, committing 14 more bank robberies before being caught after holding up two Oklahoma banks in the same day. Sentenced to 25 years in federal prison at McAlester, Oklahoma, he was paroled after serving less than four. From McAlester, Starr moved to Claremore, where he once again reverted to his old ways. He and two accomplices held up an Arkansas bank, using a Nash motorcar instead of a horse in an attempt to get away. However, it was one bank robbery too many for Henry Starr. He was shot in the back by bank president William Myers, who had a shotgun hidden in the vault. At a nearby jail, doctors removed pellets from Starr's spine. However, he died from the wound four days later, on February 22, 1921. His wife, his mother, and his 17-year-old son were by his side. Thanks to a gift to J.M. Davis, Starr's notorious connection to Claremore did not end with his death. The outlaw had earlier been arrested near Lake Charles, Louisiana, by Deputy Sheriff H.S. Holliday. When released, Starr promised the officer he would arrange it so Holliday could obtain one of his guns. The promise was kept when Starr's sister presented Holliday with a .38 Colt revolver. Holliday later gave the weapon to Davis to add to his growing collection. The revolver is on display at the museum.

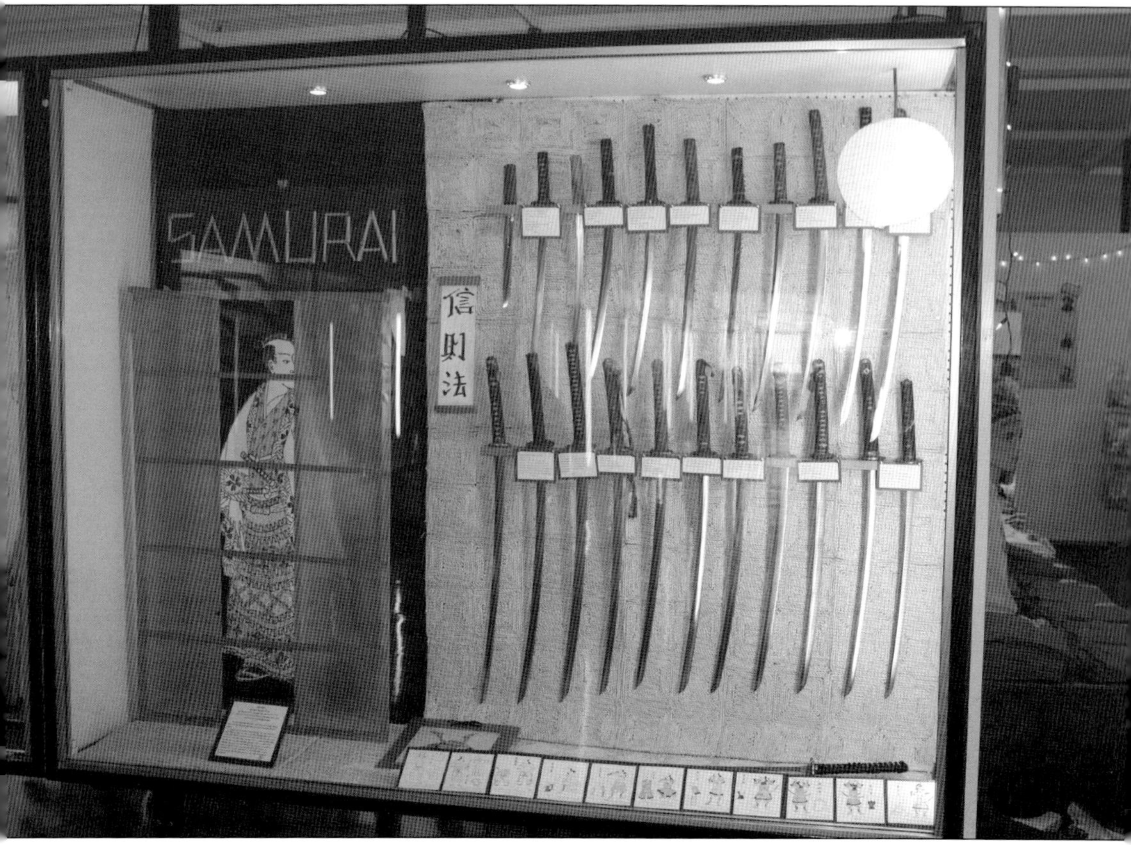

Davis acquired a great portion of his collection from returning servicemen after both World War I and World War II. Many of these items were firearms, but not all of them were. One item that was very much sought after by soldiers and Marines serving in the Pacific Theater of World War II was the Japanese samurai sword. Japanese officers were allowed to carry a sword as a badge of their rank. Some of these swords were a standard military issue, but many were not. Japan's historic warrior culture was centered on the samurai, the servant warrior with his spirit-endowed, sharper-than-razor-sharp sword. The sword was so important to the samurai that blades were passed down from generation to generation in a noble family. Many Japanese officers in the 1930s and 1940s took their family's treasured sword blade into battle. They would have the blade re-hilted to match or closely resemble the contemporary military hilt. Just as American culture celebrates the mythic cowboy with his Colt .45 revolver on his hip, the Japanese samurai, with his long curved sword, was a myth-shrouded icon. American soldiers knew this, too. What better war trophy to bring back to the states than the "soul" of a defeated enemy—the sword, the soul, of a samurai. Over the years, J.M Davis collected many Japanese swords and knives. These either came from the soldier who actually collected it, or from someone who had previously gathered it from a soldier.

Thompson SMG
Invented By John T. Thompson, 1919

No single firearm better exemplifies the Roaring Twenties than the Thompson submachine gun. The "Tommy Gun," as it became widely known, was designed by John T. Thompson in 1919. It fires the same .45 Automatic Colt Pistol cartridge, highly regarded for its "man-stopping" ability, used in the famed Model 1911 pistol. The Thompson was sought after by soldiers, law enforcement officers, and criminals from the 1920s onward. Depending upon the model, the Thompson could spray out between 600 to 1,000 rounds per minute, a fact that helped it acquire such nicknames as "chopper," "Chicago typewriter," and "trench broom."

Colt .38 Automatic

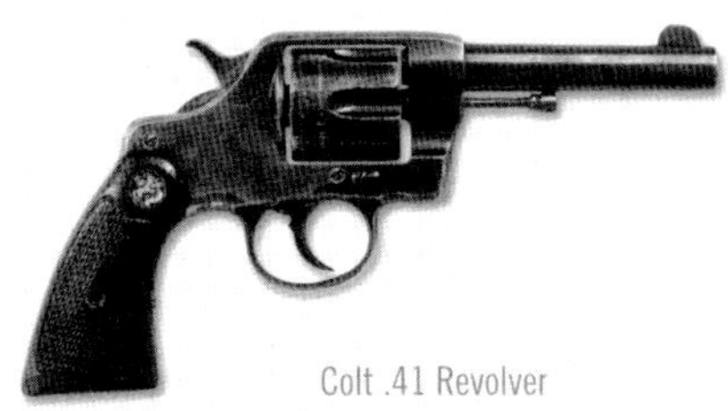

Colt .41 Revolver

Colt .38 Automatic

Most outlaws and other bad guys from America's past did not have one particular gun they used throughout their careers in crime. Often, these guys (and some gals) used a gun for a particular crime and then ditched it, stealing or buying another one for their next job. Since many of them were well known to the law enforcement community, it was better for them not to have a recently fired gun on them, just in case forces of the law detained them. This is probably the reason the J.M. Davis Museum has six firearms attributed to the career of Charlie "Pretty Boy" Floyd: two short-barreled shotguns, two revolvers, and two semi-automatic pistols. One of the semi-automatics seems to be more than a throwaway. When a former curator was performing routine care for the pistol, he found what appears to be an escape map carved into the underside of one of the hard-plastic grip panels.

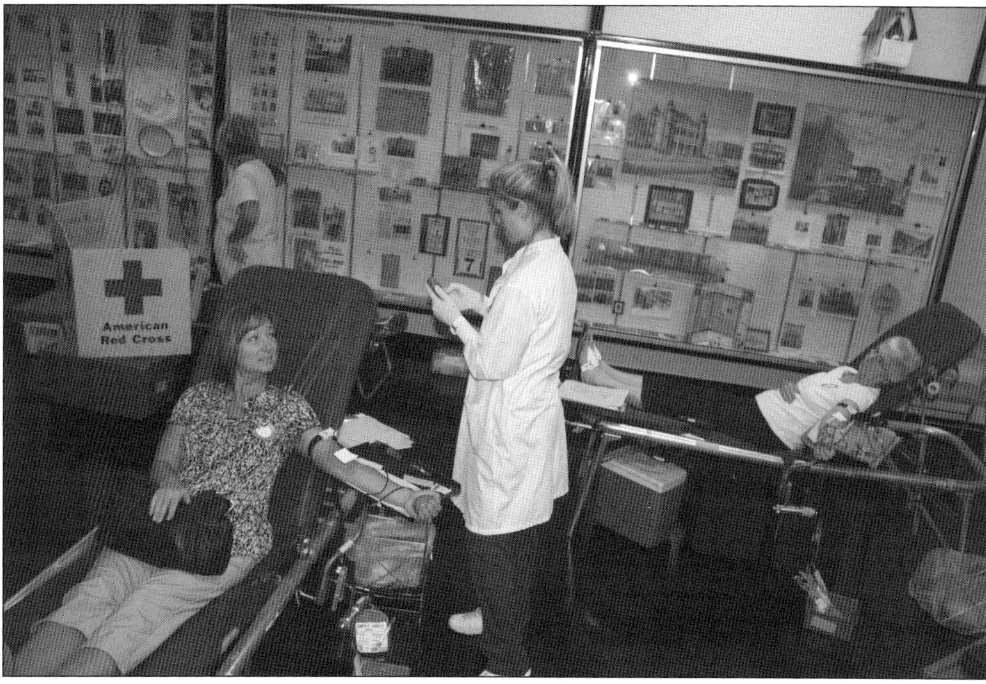

The Davis Museum is open to many community events. The American Red Cross sets up twice a year for a blood drive in the Claremore Room. The Davis Museum often exceeds its goal for units collected.

During the popular Claremore Rodeo, the rodeo queen contestants make an appearance at the Davis Museum. Among those on hand in 2011 were Miss Rodeo Oklahoma Princess 2011, Baileigh Warren (left), of Collinsville, Oklahoma; and Miss Rodeo Oklahoma 2011, Jamie Virden, of Marlow, Oklahoma.

A new exhibit opened in 2010 to highlight the background and the planning of the J.M. Davis Arms and Historical Museum in the late 1960s. A ribbon-cutting ceremony was held to open the new exhibit. From left to right are Jason Schubert, Davis Museum curator; Tad Jones, Oklahoma state representative; Sean Burrage, Oklahoma senator; Donna McSpadden, wife of former Oklahoma state senate pro tem Clem McSpadden, who spearheaded the drive to build the museum; and Wayne McCombs, Davis Museum executive director.

Along with the founding of the museum exhibit, Leslie McLaughlin of Skiatook, Oklahoma, completed a mural of the Mason Hotel (1910–1986). Davis housed his collection in the hotel until the museum was built in 1969.

The museum's ability to serve the needs of the public got a big boost in May 2017, when RCB Bank supplied its staff with two servers, six desktop computers, and a laptop computer. Seen here with curator Jason Schubert (center) are, from left to right, RCB Bank representatives Mike Anderson, senior vice president of technology; Tom Krause, server administrator; Matt Mason, RCB Bank-Claremore market president; and Sara Moss, customer and community relations officer.

In February 2011, the J.M. Davis Museum opened an exhibit on Operation Iraqi Freedom, using material and information from retired Marine M.Sgt. Dale Marsh, an Iraq veteran. "They have World War I, World War II, Korea and definitely Vietnam [at the museum]," Marsh told the *Tulsa World's* Rhett Morgan. "I wanted to see something for the current guys." The display includes an Iraqi Republican Guard "Darth Vader" helmet.

Famed vocalist and Claremore native Patti Page poses before her Claremore Wall of Fame portrait in this 2010 photograph. Page sold more records than any other female singer in the decade of the 1950s. Her plaque sits between one of Clem McSpadden, the famous rodeo announcer and politician who was instrumental in getting the museum established, and Andy Payne, winner of the 1920s transcontinental foot race known as the Bunion Derby, on a wall of the J.M. Davis Museum.

On April 26, 2010, the initial 10 honorees into the Claremore Wall Fame were revealed to the public. Each of the men and women pictured on the wall were people with strong Claremore ties who had distinguished themselves in their chosen fields. They included, from left to right, J.M. Davis, represented here by his nephew Bill Higgins; former J.C. Penny CEO W.R. Howell, represented by his niece Cheryl Askew, sister Jerry Brasier, and nephew Hal Brasier; rodeo announcer, state senator and US Congressman Clem McSpadden, represented by his wife Donna; athlete Andy Payne, represented by nephew Gerry Payne and his wife Shirley; playwright Lynn Riggs, represented by Fran Jones of the Rogers County Historical Society; Clem Rogers and son Will Rogers, represented by Doris "Coke" Meyer, great-granddaughter of Clem and great-niece of Will; astronaut Stuart Roosa, wife of his brother Dan and Jeanette Parker and niece of Stuart Roosa; and philanthropist Helen Walton, represented by her sister-in-law Ludmila Robson and Helen's brother Frank Robson.

Thanks to the Claremore-based Pelco Structural, LLC, the museum has a continuously playing video display of Claremore Hall of Fame inductees. Beginning as the Claremore Wall of Fame, the name was changed in 2016 to reflect the video component made possible by Pelco.

Shirley Jones, movie and TV star, broke into films with *Oklahoma!* in 1955. She visited the Davis Museum in 2011, when her *Oklahoma!* character, Laurey Williams, was inducted into the Claremore Wall of Fame. Here she poses with museum director Wayne McCombs in the movie's famous "Surrey with the Fringe on Top."

Washington, DC-based Cyrus Avery II (center), along with daughter Allyson and son Cyrus III, visited the museum in June 2011, taking special interest in the Route 66 mural, which features a portrait of the first Cyrus Avery. Dubbed "The Father of Route 66," Tulsa businessman Avery pushed for the creation of a highway between Chicago and Los Angeles in the early 1920s. The original Highway 66 lies just west of the museum, with the new Route 66 running to its east.

The world-famous Main Street of America, Route 66, is known today for its many roadside attractions and the constant stream of tourists and others who take to the venerable highway at some point between Chicago and Los Angeles. Also known as the Mother Road, it runs right by the Davis Museum, and since 1969, when the museum's doors first opened, untold thousands of Route 66 travelers have visited the Davis collection. A good portion of them do not leave until they have taken pictures of themselves with the sign on the museum's west side—a perfect Mother Road "photo op."

Like many other longtime Claremore residents, Jim Batchelder first encountered J.M. Davis's collection as a youngster, when Davis had it displayed throughout his Mason Hotel. And from the beginning, Batchelder was hooked. "The first time I went in there I was probably 12 years old, and after that, I couldn't stay away," he recalls. "I think I was around 15 years old when I first got permission from mom and dad to go down there by myself. The hotel just fascinated me. I was so fascinated that I couldn't keep my mind off of it." He remembers warming up to Davis almost immediately, and vice versa. Perhaps the fact that Davis had been a sickly child led to the special bond between him and young Batchelder, who was afflicted with cerebral palsy. "One day he told me he didn't want to say anything out of the way, but he noticed how I walked and stuff, and he asked me what was wrong. I told him, and he said, 'Well, you sure have a lot of ambition. Would you consider helping me with the elevator and the people coming in?'" So, at the age of 18, Batchelder became the Mason Hotel's elevator operator and "kind of a semi-guide" for visitors, sharing his knowledge and love of the collection. He did that for three years before taking a job as a reserve deputy sheriff. But even though he was no longer an employee, he continued to spend as much time as he could with Davis and his artifacts. "It hurt me real bad when he passed," Batchelder says, "But I never lost my love for what he'd done. I'm thankful that the state stepped in and did this museum, because it gives other children a chance to grow up with some the things I grew up with." "To me," he adds, "just being able to meet him was the highest honor. Wow. Even as old as I am now (70), I can't put into words how that all made me feel."

It has been a few years since J.M. Davis Memorial Commission member Rick Mosier graduated from Claremore High School. But even now, if the Claremore lawyer sees visitors putting their hands or noses on the glass display cases at the Davis Museum, he feels a twinge of distress that sends him back to the summer of 1974. Mosier was between his sophomore and junior year of high school when he secured a summer job as a gofer at the museum. "When anyone needed something, I was the one to go for it," he explains. "I was really at the bottom of the totem pole on the museum staff." Although he helped assemble many of the museum's display cases, his main job was maintenance, sweeping the floor and cleaning the glass cases. "I learned a lot about hand and nose prints left by visitors trying to get a good look at the artifacts on display and cleaned a lot of dirty streaks left about three feet high by younger visitors more interested in just running down the aisles," he remembers. "I spent hours cleaning the glass and wiping those prints off." However, he adds, "It was a great summer job for a 16-year-old and paid well at $2.25 per hour." The young man who took that entry-level position at the museum so many years ago was appointed by Oklahoma's governor in 2018 to serve as one of the museum's commissioners. He replaced Associate District Judge Jack Mayberry, who had retired from the board. Many years before his summer job, Mosier had become intrigued by the kinds of artifacts that are featured in the J.M. Davis collection. "My fourth grade teacher, Mrs. Brown, was a Civil War buff and had a collection of items carried by her grandfather during the war," he recalls. "One day she brought an 1863 Sharps .52 caliber carbine and I was hooked. She arranged for us to purchase Minié balls [bullets] that had been excavated from Civil War battlefields. I still have mine." Another rifle that interests Mosier is the Model 1873 Winchester, marketed by the manufacturer as "the gun that won the West." His great-great-grandfather purchased one in San Francisco and carried it with him while bringing his family and a herd of horses over the Rocky Mountains to Kansas. The family still owns the rifle. "These memories are the reason I wanted to serve on the Davis Commission," he says. "We can teach younger generations so much about the history of our nation and the people who forged it and protected it through the display of Mr. Davis's collection."

Among the rare and important firearms on display at the museum is this Colt Single Action Army Revolver, which is believed to have been the property of famed Territorial lawman Bill Tilghman, who was not only one of the leading area lawmen in the late 19th and early 20th centuries, but also a pioneering Oklahoma filmmaker. J.M. Davis purchased this weapon from Merle A. Gill, a Kansas City–based ballistics expert, in 1948, along with several other pieces; its serial number indicates that it was manufactured in 1902. At the time, Gill said that he'd purchased it from Tilghman himself, who was shot to death by a corrupt Prohibition officer on the streets of Cromwell, Oklahoma, in 1924.

The Mason Hotel exhibit in the museum includes the oldest firearm in the J.M Davis collection: a c. 1350 Chinese hand cannon. Basically a bronze tube with one end blocked, it was fired by lighting a cloth wick that was stuffed into the hole at the rear. It may seem primitive and ineffective today, but its death-dealing .90 caliber metal projectile was vastly superior to the swords, bows and arrows, and spears of its day.

The Cherokee Nation donated $10,000 to the Davis Museum in 2018 for curatorial supplies and assistance on a new Cherokee Nation display that opened in April 2019. District 14 Cherokee Nation Tribal Council member Keith Austin (left) looks over some of the supplies that were used in preparing the new Cherokee display.

The Davis Museum has participated each year as one of the city's representatives in Claremore Day at the Oklahoma State Capitol. The Daisy BB gun gallery is a very popular stop for visitors at the Claremore exhibition. In 2014, from left to right, Rogers County senator Sean Burrage, Lt. Gov. Todd Lamb, and state representative Marty Quinn challenged each other's shooting skills.

State representative Carl Newton, holding the rifle, was the marksmanship champion in 2018. Claremore Navy Junior Reserve Officers' Training Corps cadets Kartina Sherrick and Seth Sanders assisted in range safety. Newton represents District 58, which includes Alfalfa, Major, Woods, and Woodward Counties.

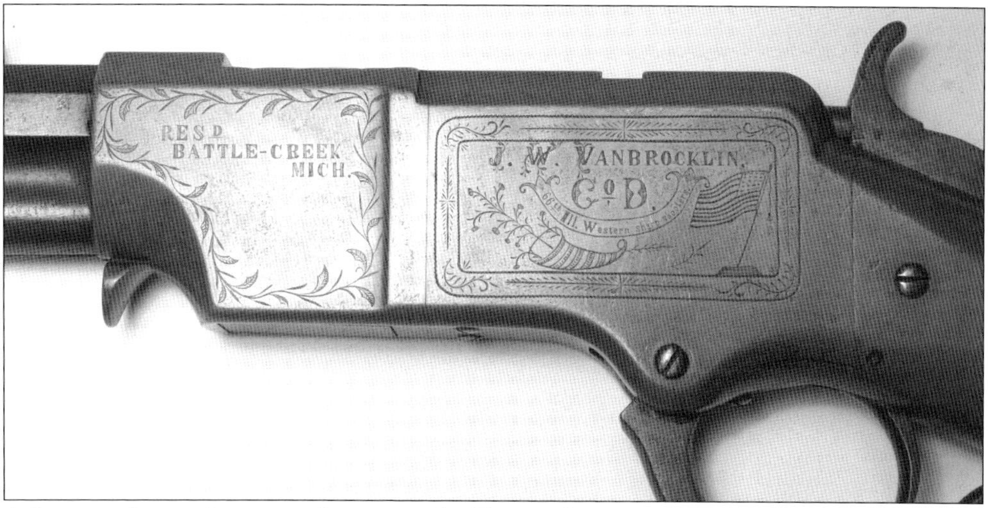

A favorite of many firearm enthusiasts is the Henry rifle. It is a .44 caliber rim fire lever action rifle designed by the New Haven Arms Company's shop foreman B. Tyler Henry. It could hold 16 self-contained cartridges in its tubular magazine. In the hands of Union sharpshooters, it caused Confederate soldiers to call it the Yankee rifle "you load on Sunday and shoot all week." John W. Van Brocklin, of Battle Creek, Michigan, a Union sharpshooter during the Civil War, originally owned the only Henry in the J.M. Davis Museum collection. Van Brocklin's Henry rifle bears the serial number 2523. At an additional expense, he had it engraved. Included in the panel and floral engraving on the left side of the receiver is the name "J.W. Van Brocklin, Co. D. 66th Ill. Western Sharpshooters, RESd [reside] Battle-Creek, Mich." The right of the receiver is engraved with the stars and stripes and an eagle holding a banner reading, "Death to Traitors."

The J.M. Davis Foundation, Inc., was formed "for the purpose of preserving for posterity the varied collections of J.M. Davis, including but not limited to guns, steins, statuary, musical instruments, saddles, horns, Indian and Western Lore and other artifacts; to provide for free public display the collections aforesaid in the City of Claremore, Rogers County, State of Oklahoma, being the residence and domicile of said J.M. Davis." Toward those ends, the foundation entrusted the collections to the State of Oklahoma under a 99-year lease, with the foundation continuing to monitor the display and care of the collections. Pictured is Claremore attorney Larry Rahmeier, who serves as a trustee and secretary-treasurer.

This particular Adams revolver once belonged to Tandy Walker, colonel of the Confederate States Army's first regiment of Choctaw and Chickasaw mounted rifles. The iron plate at the butt of the grip is engraved "Col. Tandy Walker, Indian Brigade". He, too, occupied an influential position in the councils of the tribe after its settlement in the west. He was the first principal chief, or governor, of the Choctaw Nation under the Skullyville Constitution in Indian Territory (current day eastern Oklahoma). At the outbreak of the Civil War, he entered the confederate military service in the first regiment of Choctaw and Chickasaw Mounted Rifles. He became lieutenant colonel of that unit, and on the promotion of its colonel, Douglas H. Cooper, to the grade of brigadier general, Tandy succeeded to the command of the regiment with the rank of colonel. Upon the organization of the Indian Territory Troops into the Indian Division under the command of General Cooper, Colonel Walker was given command of the Second Indian Cavalry Brigade in which position he distinguished himself as a capable leader. After the war, He returned to his home in Skullyville, where he later died on February 2, 1877.

The J.M. Davis Museum's executive directors, past and present, are as follows: Benny Garren, 1967–1970; Pearl Golden, 1970–1974; Sue Cook, 1974–1989; and Lee Good, 1989–1998. Pictured in the first row, from left to right, are Duane Kyler, 2001–2005; Shirley Johnson, 1998–2001; and John Cummins, 2005–2007. In the second row, from left to right, are Gary Rhor, 2007–2008; Wayne McCombs, 2009–present; and Jason Schubert, who served twice as interim director, in 2007 and 2008–2009.

As the saying goes, choose a job you love and you will never work a day in your life. That is how Pat Cameron feels about greeting visitors daily at the J.M. Davis Arms and Historical Museum. While she is assigned a wide assortment of duties, what she relishes the most is having the opportunity to meet all the guests that come through the doors. "We have had residents from all 50 states and from around the world," Pat says with pride. "There are many times we may not be able to speak the same language, but that's never a real problem. It is clear they are enjoying their stay." Following retirement in the 1980s, Pat and her husband, Bracken, moved from Tulsa to Claremore. While her husband quickly took to the nonworking lifestyle, Pat decided she was not quite ready to be a full-time homebody. "I am a people person. My husband knew this. He and his friends met at the donut shop each morning. We agreed I needed something new also. I started looking for a job." In 1989, she found it, joining the Davis staff. "I have always enjoyed history," she notes, "so what better place to work than at a museum?" With her extensive knowledge of the exhibits, Pat is a great resource for visitors. She can explain, for example, that the collection's oldest weapon is a Chinese hand cannon from 1350. If she is pinned down about her favorite part of the museum, Pat will say it is the numerous John Rogers statues on display. "His plaster models have so much remarkable detail," she explains. "I had read about the 19th-century artist but never saw one of his works until I started here." In addition to sharing her love for the museum, Pat gets to hear numerous personal stories from visitors. "Someone is always finding something a family member may have owned or one like it. Some of the tales are funny; some are lonely and a bit sad. All are touching. And once, I was even invited by a gentleman to go square-dancing with him," Pat admits with a laugh.

When you are born and raised in Claremore, Oklahoma, and continue to make your home there, it is impossible for you not to know about J.M. Davis and his Mason Hotel, as well as Davis's massive displays of weapons and other artifacts. After Davis saw his collection moved to a new home, the J.M. Davis Arms and Historical Museum, the old hotel was ultimately razed. Now, it exists only in memories—including those of museum employee Shirley McClurg. "I cannot count the times my family would take guests to first the hotel and then later the museum," she says. "Never once did I think I would be working there." McClurg is one of those lifelong Claremore citizens. And for the past 22 years, she has also been one of the friendly staff members who welcome visitors to the museum. "I really like meeting all the interesting people that stop here," says McClurg. "They come from all over." In addition to being a greeter, she has several other duties at the museum. She admits that she was not exactly sure what job she was applying for back in 1997, when she joined her friend Pat Cameron on the staff. "Pat actually was the one who told me I should come to work at the museum," McClurg remembers. "We had met at the beauty shop." At the time she took the position, she was a retiree, having worked for 28 years as a secretary and registrar for Oklahoma Military Academy, seeing the institution through its transition to Claremore Junior College (now Rogers State University). "It didn't take long for me to realize I needed to keep busy," McClurg notes. "I saw an employment want ad in the [*Claremore*] *Progress* and I answered it. Lee Good was the director. The newspaper ad didn't list what they needed, but apparently he felt I could fit in. I asked when my first day would be and he said the following day." Over the years, she has worked for six directors. In addition to greeting visitors each day, her duties include serving in the gift shop, answering the telephone, handling office paperwork, and other tasks. But it is the joy of visiting with the guests that gives McClurg the most satisfaction. She especially enjoys it when something out of the ordinary takes place. For instance, she remembers a couple walking in one afternoon and asking the whereabouts of a certain artifact. They had a brief conversation, and she directed them to the display. As they were preparing to leave, another employee walked up and said, "Oh Shirley, I see you have met Garth Brooks and Trisha Yearwood."

In 2011, the Outdoor Channel began producing a new television show that featured information, experiences, and operations of specific firearms for each episode. Called *Gun Stories*, it featured veteran movie and television actor Joe Mantegna as host. With the company producing *Gun Stories*, Winnercomm, located just down the road in Tulsa, the show's producer-director came to Claremore looking for guns and information. Luckily, the J.M. Davis Museum had both. The Museum held an example of nearly every firearm the show wanted to feature that first season, and curator Jason Schubert became one of the show's interviewees. During the filming of the seventh season of *Gun Stories*, the entire production crew and Mantegna traveled to Claremore, with many of Mantegna's segment-introduction scenes for that season shot in the aisles of the J.M. Davis Museum. After filming in the museum, the crew headed to Krebs, Oklahoma, for an episode centered around the Winchester 1897 pump shotgun owned by Mantegna's grandfather, who had emigrated with two of his best friends from Sicily to mine coal around McAlester, Oklahoma. The three men purchased a parcel of land from the Choctaw Nation and homesteaded there. The program was shot on the old Mantegna farm, which is still owned by the descendants of one of Mantegna's grandfather's fellow immigrants.

The Maltese Falcon is one of America's greatest films and probably the most famous film noir movie ever made. In it, Sam Spade is not only trying to find the eponymous black bird but is also seeking the person who murdered his private investigator partner Miles Archer. Spade says that Archer's murderer used a Webley-Fosbery automatic revolver. So, what is an automatic revolver, and why would someone want one? It is a revolver that automatically cocks itself for the next shot each time it is fired. A (semi-)automatic pistol has a part that slides back and ejects the spent brass case when it is fired, then that part slides back and loads a new cartridge into the barrel, ready to be fired. The Webley-Fosbery's barrel and cylinder, however, slide back during firing, with the rearward motion causing the cylinder to rotate to line up a new cartridge for firing. It also cocks the hammer. The spent, fired, empty brass case stays in the cylinder, just as in a normal revolver. World War I–era combat airplane pilots liked this feature because getting hot brass down a flight jacket did not help one successfully fly a canvas-covered flying wooden crate. After all the Webley-Fosbery's cartridges are fired, the operator pushes a lever that makes the barrel and cylinder hinge forward, offering quick control of the spent cartridge's ejection. There are three of these very interesting automatic revolvers on display at the J.M. Davis Arms and Historical Museum.

There are very few firearms more recognized than the Walther PPK. Not everyone may know what a Walther PPK is, what caliber it is, or what separates it from a Walther PP, but almost everyone knows who uses a Walther PPK. It is Ian Fleming's licensed-to-kill British Secret Service agent 007—Bond, James Bond. Bond's Walther PPK, chambered in .32ACP (7.65mm), was first introduced in the book and movie *Dr. No*. Today's Bond, Daniel Craig, uses a Walther PPK/S in .380 ACP (9mm Short, Kurz, 9x17mm). In 1929, Walther, of Germany, developed a slim semi-automatic handgun that it marketed to law enforcement. The company called it the *Politzeipistole* (Police Pistol), or PP for short. The next year, Walther shortened the barrel by .6 inch and the grip by .4 inch to make a smaller package suitable for concealed carry by plainclothes officers, or *Kriminal*, as the Germans called detectives and inspectors. With the addition of "K" (for *Kriminal*) to PP, the PPK was born. By today's standards (or prejudices), these cartridges are all pretty weak for self-defense. However, a 1929 European lawman's needs were a far cry from those of San Francisco police inspector Harry Callahan, as played by Clint Eastwood in the 1971 hit movie *Dirty Harry*. He used a .44 Mangum, which he (erroneously) calls "the most powerful handgun in the world." Weak cartridges or not, however, everyone knows 007 is such an amazing super-spy that he always hits what he aims for. Don't shot placement and wry comments always drop the bad guy?

In the winter of 2018, students from Northeast Technology Center, Claremore, produced a series of radio and television spots promoting the museum's 50th anniversary. Oklahoma's newly elected lieutenant governor, Matt Pinnell, was selected to be the spokesman for the commercials. From left to right are student Charles Keely, Lt. Gov. Matt Pinnell, student Matthew Johnson, and Davis Museum executive director Wayne McCombs.

As chairman of the J.M. Davis Memorial Commission, Claremore attorney William R. Higgins is proud of and pleased by how the Davis collection is housed and displayed today. He feels that J.M. and his first wife, Addie, would be proud of the museum that bears Mr. Davis's name. But sometime, he thinks of the collection in a different way, seeing it through the eyes of an adolescent boy in the late 1950s, given free rein to wander through the lobby and halls of the Mason Hotel, where Davis's treasures were then housed. To him, the owners of the hotel were not Mr. and Mrs. Davis; they were Uncle Monroe and Aunt Addie. "It wasn't like my friends and I ran wild up and down the halls," Higgins recalls. "I knew better than to do anything like that." His parents, Bob and Denyse, operated the Mason Hotel Coffee Shop. Separated from the hotel lobby by an impressive archway, the café's walls were covered from floor to ceiling with items from J.M. Davis's collection—just like the rest of the establishment. Higgins remembers Uncle Monroe allowing him to enter some of the rooms on the building's second and third floors that were closed to the public, where he saw countless boxes of weapons and other items that could not be displayed because of lack of space. "I also remember [that] my uncle would allow me to help him in his workshop. Actually, I'm pretty sure it was more like him making me believe I was helping," he notes. Like other children, William and his younger sister, Kathy, always looked forward to Christmas. With it, however, came a seasonal task most kids would never have dreamed of doing. "It was impossible in the rest of the hotel, due to the numbers, but all the guns in the café area and banquet room were taken down and dusted and cleaned. We did it every year during the Christmas break from school," he explains. "I believe my father being a retired US Army sergeant major may have had something to do with this." Because of his unique awareness of what the collection meant to J.M. and Addie Davis, Higgins is especially honored to serve as the commission's chairman. "I know my uncle and aunt would be pleased by how the collection is on display at the museum," he says. "It was his longtime wish for a place to share his collection. Our facilities continue to improve and are in better shape than ever. Of course, we will continue to need more operating capital, but we are headed in the right direction."

As a state agency, the J.M. Davis Arms and Historical Museum is governed by a five-person board, with each member appointed by the Oklahoma governor and approved by the Oklahoma State Senate. In January 2019, the Davis Museum's commissioners were, from left to right, (sitting) Rick Mosier and William Higgins, commission chairman; (standing) Dr. Keith Ballard, Hays Gilstrap, and Denny Haddox.

The Friends of the J.M. Davis Museum, Inc., enlist support for the preservation of the memory of J.M. Davis and the promotion the future of the J.M. Davis Arms and Historical Museum. Formed in 2009, the organization has provided funds for dozens of museum projects, including the Daisy BB indoor shooting gallery, outside beautification projects, the sealing of the museum's parking lot, the dedication of the outdoor tank bench, transportation to tourism and professional-development conventions, and the marble enclosure for the museum's time capsule. Claremore resident Matt Tarvin is president of this invaluable group.

In 2015, country music superstar and Checotah, Oklahoma, native Carrie Underwood released a new single called "Little Toy Gun." To promote it, her record label sent water pistols carrying the song's title to radio stations across the country. Two years later, at a concert by Underwood in Tulsa, Matt Bradley, morning personality at KWEN radio, had her sign a photo for the Davis Museum and donated the toy pistol to go along with it. Both now can be seen in a museum display featuring many other toys in the Davis collection, including cap guns, pop guns, and water pistols.

John Wooley (left) is an Oklahoma-based author, journalist, editor, and broadcaster who has written extensively about the state's popular culture. His 2011 book *Shot in Oklahoma* received the Outstanding Book on Oklahoma History Award from the Oklahoma Historical Society. His work at the *Tulsa World* newspaper, where he spent 23 years as an entertainment writer, won major awards from the Associated Press and Society of Professional Journalists. In 2003, he became the first writer to be inducted into the Oklahoma Music Hall of Fame. Larry Larkin (center), a Claremore resident since 1963, is a lifelong fan of movie and television Westerns. An admirer of the Davis collection since seeing it for the first time as a seven-year-old in the Mason Hotel, he has been a newspaper and magazine correspondent writing mainly historical articles for the past 20 years. He is the former sports editor of the *Claremore Progress* and a correspondent for both the *Tulsa World* and *Tulsa Tribune*. Larkin is a collector of western movie and TV memorabilia as well as comic books. Wayne McCombs (right) is the executive director of the J.M. Davis Arms and Historical Museum. He has a 40-year background in advertising, broadcasting, and public relations. He has authored and coauthored five books about baseball in Oklahoma. He is a member of the University of Tulsa Athletic Hall of Fame committee.

Discover Thousands of Local History Books Featuring Millions of Vintage Images

Arcadia Publishing, the leading local history publisher in the United States, is committed to making history accessible and meaningful through publishing books that celebrate and preserve the heritage of America's people and places.

Find more books like this at
www.arcadiapublishing.com

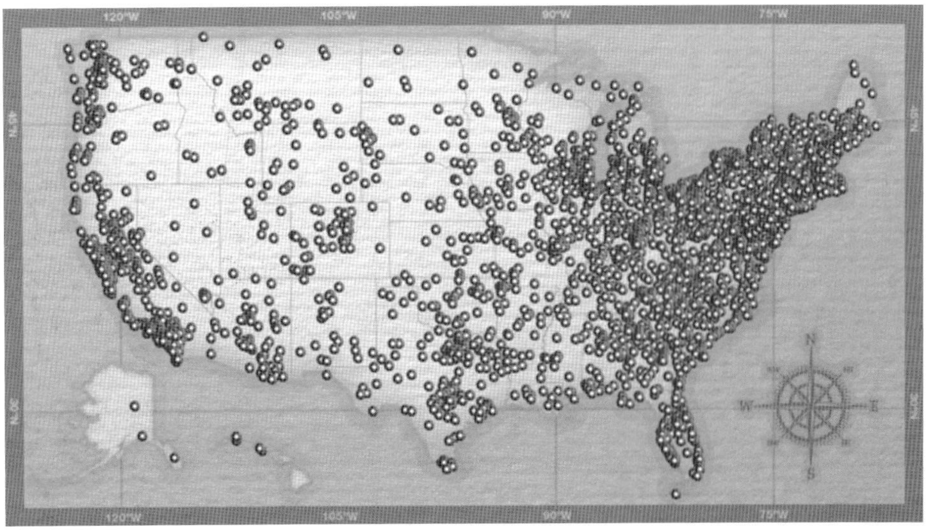

Search for your hometown history, your old stomping grounds, and even your favorite sports team.

Consistent with our mission to preserve history on a local level, this book was printed in South Carolina on American-made paper and manufactured entirely in the United States. Products carrying the accredited Forest Stewardship Council (FSC) label are printed on 100 percent FSC-certified paper.

MADE IN THE USA